A

Prophetic Manifesto

FOR THE NEW ERA

DESTINY IMAGE BOOKS BY PATRICIA KING

The Glory Has Come

Arise

Spiritual Revolution

Light Belongs in the Darkness

So You Want to Change the World?

A

Prophetic
Manifesto

FOR THE NEW ERA

20

PROPHETIC WORDS
FOR THE 2020S

PATRICIA KING

DESTINY IMAGE® PUBLISHERS, INC.

P.O. Box 310, Shippensburg, PA 17257-0310

"Promoting Inspired Lives."

This book and all other Destiny Image and Destiny Image Fiction books are available at Christian bookstores and distributors worldwide.

Cover design by Eileen Rockwell
Interior design by Terry Clifton

For more information on foreign distributors, call 717-532-3040.

Reach us on the Internet: www.destinyimage.com.

ISBN 13 TP: 978-0-7684-5630-1
ISBN 13 eBook: 978-0-7684-5631-8
ISBN 13 HC: 978-0-7684-5633-2
ISBN 13 LP: 978-0-7684-5632-5

For Worldwide Distribution, Printed in the U.S.A.
1 2 3 4 5 6 7 8 / 24 23 22 21 20

CONTENTS

FOREWORD

by James W. Goll

Jesus taught us that we need new wine skins to hold the new wine. Without riverbanks, the teeming current of life can become nothing more than run-off water and even worse, forms into a flood plain. When good boundaries are put in place and adequately communicated and applied, this in turn creates what I call a "Safe House." Too often—in church history and in recent times—the prophetic movement has tended to create a few messes. This could partially happen because we need to review ethical guidelines and protocols that are necessary for prophetic maturation—and even update these principles from time to time.

On Passover of 2020, late at night, I was worshipping the Lord in my backyard. As I was, the clear voice of the Lord came to me saying, *"I have been waiting for such a long time for My people to slow down long enough so they can hear what I have to say in this hour. I have much I want to share concerning the new ways for the new era and the new wine skins for the new wine. Will you be like Moses and turn aside? I AM waiting there!"* This word has personally pierced my being and set me on a path to make sure that in my own life I am not letting gifting or pressures of life and ministry distract me from getting in God's face. If we ever need to "turn aside" to hear a clear word from the Lord, it is in these times.

I have had a friendship and functioned in an advisory role to Patricia King and her vital ministry for several years now. I know her well and consider it a great honor to walk with her and Ron, her strong, supportive husband. Patricia is as effective as she is because she lives her revelation. Her word is her bond. She has also chosen to surround herself with godly relationships in both apostolic alignment, great staff, and warring intercessors.

With this background and knowledge, Patricia King is perfectly positioned to release this book, *A Prophetic Manifesto for the New Era*, which you now hold in your hands. Thank you, Patricia, for helping identify the riverbanks of God and provide proper protocol to help propel the prophetic movement into great effectiveness and maturity.

With gratitude,

DR. JAMES W. GOLL
Founder of God Encounters Ministries
GOLL Ideation LLC

FOREWORD

By Lana Vawser

In this hour we are in, where there is a major shift taking place, it is imperative that we are people that hear what the Spirit of God is saying to His people. Quite a number of years ago I heard the Lord say in a dream "It's not the end of a season, Lana, it's the end of an era." As I woke, I knew that the Lord was speaking that as the Church we were coming to a time where we were about to enter a new era. We have now entered that new area and the striking thing about a new era is, it is completely new (Isaiah 43:19). I remember the Lord speaking to me so clearly a while ago and He said, "You have not been this way before."

So here we are, in a completely new era, a time in the earth where we have "not been this way before," it's uncharted territory and it is a time to really lean close to His heart and hear His voice.

In a new era, there are new strategies, new blueprints, new wine-skins, and new pathways. What takes place in that time is unlike anything we have seen before and what is going to take place in this new era, we have not seen before.

In this completely new time, in this time of major transition, shifting, and change, we must be people that recognize the times and the seasons like the sons of Issachar and have tender hearts toward the Lord and what He is doing. I have been feeling very strongly that we are to draw close to the Lord in this hour and to cry out like David in Psalm 25:4 *"Make me to know your ways, O LORD; teach me your paths."* We are also to be the Church that arises in this new era that is receiving the wisdom of God and prophetic solutions as we navigate things in the earth that we have not seen before.

This book that you hold in your hand right now is a gift to you and a gift to the Church. Patricia King has had such a significant impact on my life as a woman who carries the heart of the Lord, carries His revelation and wisdom, and is truly a friend of God. She is a woman after His own heart, and a woman of such integrity and character.

What you hold in your hand right now is not just a "book", it is a road map. It is a divine GPS for this new era to help you navigate what the Lord is going to do. This is a book to marinate in. This is not just a book; it is the revelation of Heaven. At the end of every chapter there are thoughts to ponder and prayers that I strongly encourage you to take your time to make your way through, as I believe that there is significant encounter, impartation, mani-festation, and revelation that the Spirit of God is going to release to you.

These pages are going to prepare you for the days ahead. As I read through these pages, I was undone by how much God loves His Church. Patricia has articulated His heart and His tone with such purity and accuracy. The pages drip in the heartbeat of a loving Father to bring His Church into alignment and call her into position. The Lord loves His people so much that He is cleaning house and inviting us into deeper alignment with Him and His ways, so we can partner with Him in the glorious unveiling of His Majesty and Glory that is going to be revealed in the earth in this hour. This book is a tool to keep in your toolbelt and to refer back to over and over in this new era.

This book is not only a gift, it's a game changer. You will be marked by the Holy Spirit through this incredible book *The Prophetic Manifesto* for the New Era to position you for the days ahead.

Lana Vawser
Author of *The Prophetic Voice of God* and
I Hear the Lord Say New Era

INTRODUCTION

Every year, during the months of July and August and through to the Day of Atonement in the fall, I posture myself to hear from the Lord regarding His purposes for the coming year. When He reveals prophetic insights, it helps me and those I serve in the Body to prepare and to position ourselves to be in found in His will for the coming months.

I found my time of seeking Him in the summer and fall of 2019 to be extremely intense and very different from other years. It became clear that the coming era would host some serious events that would demand the Body coming to attention before the Lord. The era would require a new level of consecration unto the Lord—a true focus on Jesus as shaking after shaking would ripple through the nations, confronting the idols of man. It would be an era to align, to return to the Lord, His Word, and His ways. It is an era to fear Him with awesome respect.

This book includes twenty of some of the most important and meaningful prophetic insights I received from the Lord in that season. Each chapter gives you a glimpse into God's purposes and desires for His people in this era. A great move of God's Spirit and glory, possibly the greatest we have ever known, could be encountered in this era if we, His church, align. What begins in chaos and hardship will end in glory.

Many will need the church in this era. Their hearts will fail them for fear and confusion will cloud their perception, but the people of God will be raised up as ambassadors of faith, hope, and love and will bring comfort and strength. Many souls will come into the Kingdom.

In this era:

> *Believe in the Lord your God, and you shall be established; believe His prophets, and you shall prosper* (2 Chronicles 20:20 NKJV).

Chapter *One*

AN ERA OF "NEW"

Do not call to mind the former things, or ponder things
of the past. Behold, I will do something new, now
it will spring forth; will you not be aware of it?
—ISAIAH 43:18-19

Prophecy

You have entered not only a new decade but a new era. In this coming era, you will witness much transition and you will see great glory, but also great calamity. You will see both My kindness and My severity. You will witness My judgments in the earth and the cleansing of My church. You will witness a great harvest of souls in many nations, and you will be aware of many powerful and authentic signs and wonders. You will see the emergence of a people who are lovers of Jesus and who do not fear man or are interested in what the world has to say or offer, for they are My consecrated vessels.

I am raising up a people without compromise who will carry a strong message, bringing My people back to My Word—reading it, studying it, believing it, and living it. It will be an era of great confrontation, and it will be an era that separates true believers from those who use My name only.

Great apostles, prophets, and leaders will be raised up in these days, but there will also be those whom I will remove from their place for I am bringing righteous alignment in this hour. The next seventy years shall look different from the past seventy years, but they shall be glorious and awesome years for those who draw close to Me.

It is a day and hour of tumult when lawlessness and immorality will increase and the enemy will attempt to strike with destruction. There will be an increase of wars, rumors of wars, natural disasters, and plagues but it will also be an era when righteousness will increase and when My peace, healing, and deliverance will be encountered. It is a day of separation between the wicked and the righteous for hearts will be revealed. It is an hour when you will see My grace abound where sin abounds and My standard raised against all the enemy will attempt.

This is an era for all to gaze upon My Son and to draw near without wavering. This is a new era. This era is like none other. Watch it unfold.

INSIGHTS

In the early summer of 2019, I began to prepare before the Lord for the coming season. As I sought Him for clarity, I heard the Spirit of

God reveal, *"You are entering not just a new year or a new decade, but this is the beginning of a new era."*

An era is defined as, "a long and distinct period of history with a particular feature or characteristic."[1] Over the following months as we headed into the year 2020, I heard many credible prophets confirm the new era and a number of them prophesied the exact same statement.

The year 2020 marks a new decade. In western society, when the term 20/20 is mentioned, it is usually in reference to perfect vision. The decade of the 2020s will be marked by perfect vision in the Spirit but also a sobering call to listen carefully to God's prophetic insights.

> *Put your trust in the Lord your God and you will be established. Put your trust in His prophets and succeed* (2 Chronicles 20:20).

A New Era

In order to get a glimpse of a new era, it is good to review the previous one, especially with regard to the church's activities. If we look at the last 70 years, going back to 1950, we will define an emphasis of the Spirit.

By 1950, we had just come through over 30 years of oppression and tension that included two world wars and a great depression. Israel had become a nation in 1948 and we were now seeing massive shifts in the Spirit. An era of hope, grace, and revival began with the healing movement in the '50s featuring evangelists such as Oral Roberts, William Branham, A.A Allen, Jack Coe, T.L. Osborn, and others.

In the 1960s we were introduced to the Charismatic renewal and the Jesus People Movement. God poured out great grace upon His church at that time and many were born again, filled with the Holy Spirit, and began to freely operate in the gifts of the Holy Spirit. The messianic Jewish movement was growing in this season and Christians became awakened with fresh love for the "apple of God's eye" as Israel began to flourish.

Over the decades following, we experienced a true outpouring of abundant blessing with an emphasis in the church on the unconditional love of God, His great mercies and grace, and His supernatural power. The gospel spread to the nations and believers enjoyed liberty, freedom, and prosperity. Renewals such as those in Toronto in 1994 and Brownsville in 1995 were epic and ushered in a fresh increased wave of grace and glory. Christian media exploded and began to have great impact worldwide. Emphasis on the Kingdom of God and identification with Kingdom culture filled the church. The five-fold ministry gifts with the emphasis of recognizing prophets and apostles also emerged and a worship movement emerged that gave birth to new songs and new sounds. The era was marked with grace, grace, and more grace.

While the church was enjoying refreshment in the Lord, the devil had his own track. The 1950s began to open up new mindsets in the Baby Boomer generation as they became awakened to the available freedoms. Post war, they could now dream again and come out from under the fears and restraints of the past decades. The 1960s ushered in a spiritual, sexual, and drug revolution. New Age practices were introduced *en masse* in western cultures that had previously held to foundational and traditional Christian beliefs and practices. During this season, it also became popular and acceptable to engage in sexual activities and intercourse prior to marriage and to live in uncommitted common-law unions rather than covenant marriage. The smoking of marijuana and the use of hallucinogenic drugs was also popular in the "hippie culture." The abortion reform movement began in the 1960s, and prayer and Bible reading was removed from the schools. Stores and other amenities began to open on Sundays rather than observing a national day of rest. All of this was heralded by the Baby Boomer generation in the name of "freedom."

In the following decades, traditional marriage and family practices were challenged further with the cultural norm of both parents working while children were being raised in caregiving options and the growing acceptance of same-sex marriage and transgender relationships. Sexual immorality became both rampant and blatant. At the first Superbowl of this new decade (02/02/2020), the half-time show was pornographic in that the talent dressed and danced extremely seductively and even included a pole dance formerly only to be seen in adult entertainment clubs and venues. The news report following stated that crowds overwhelmingly agreed that "the half-time show displayed the greatest athletic talent at the super bowl." As we enter the new decade, lewd behavior displayed on entertainment media and the internet has normalized sexually immoral behavior. Terrorism, murder, racism, and narcissism run rampant. What started seventy years ago as the "era of new freedom and liberty" has for the most part ended in bondage and corruption.

Even in sectors of the church, the Word was increasingly compromised to support some of the behaviors of the world.

What is God's solution? What does the new era look like? What marks it? How do we prepare? *A Prophetic Manifesto for the New Era* was written to help you discern the plans and purposes of God and then to make wise choices that will align you and prepare you for the greatest move of God ever to be seen in the history of man. Divine glory follows divine alignment. It is time to align.

Thoughts to Ponder

Do you identify with the fact that we have entered a new era?

What things that God gave us and taught us in the last era will benefit us in the new era?

Do you see signs of this transition? If so, what?

What would you like to see brought into alignment in this new era (in the world and in the church)?

What do you believe is needed in the lives of God's people in order to walk with Him in this new era?

PRAYER FOR PREPARING FOR A NEW ERA

Heavenly Father,

I thank You for all You will do in this new era. I ask You to prepare me for all that You have in store. Help me to know You in deeper ways than I have in the past and grace me to walk with You in perfect step and rhythm.

In Jesus' name I pray,

Amen.

NOTES

1. *Oxford English Dictionary*, s.v. "Era," https://www.lexico.com/en/definition/era.

Chapter
Two

An Era of Jesus Focus

We love Him because He first loved us.
—1 John 4:19 NKJV

Prophecy

Distractions, distractions, distractions! Distractions have drawn the hearts and focus of My people away from Me. Rather than walking close with Me, many are giving their attention to other meaningless things while excluding Me. They are occupied from the time they rise in the morning until the time they sleep at night. I wait and they do not come. They offer a prayer here and a prayer there, they read a scripture here and a scripture there, and worship a little here and a little there, but their hearts are far from Me. Many would rather watch a movie than spend time with Me. They would rather check their social media than engage with Me. They are more disciplined with their exercise routines and diets than they are interested in carving out time in their schedules for Me. They prefer the mundane to the holy because their hearts are distracted. They say they know Me, but where do their affections lie?

Many who serve Me in ministry have become distracted by their ministries and the assignments within them—assignments that I have not ordained but have been created due to the growth and expansion of their ministries as well as personal vision. It is time to walk away from the things that distract and return to Me.

In this hour I am addressing My people as I addressed the Church at Ephesus:

To the angel of the church of Ephesus write, "These things says He who holds the seven stars in His right hand, who walks in the midst of the seven golden lampstands: 'I know your works, your labor, your patience, and that you cannot bear those who are evil. And you have tested those who say they are apostles and are not, and have found them liars; and you have persevered and have patience, and have labored for My name's sake and have not become weary. Nevertheless I have this against you, that you have left your first love. Remember therefore from where you have fallen; repent and do the first works, or else I will come to you quickly and remove your lampstand from its place— unless you repent. But this you have, that you hate the deeds of the Nicolaitans, which I also hate. He who has an ear, let him hear what the Spirit says to the churches. To him who overcomes I will give to eat from the tree of life, which is in the midst of the Paradise of God'" (Revelation 2:1-7 NKJV).

Have you left your first love? Have you lost sight of My presence in your midst? Have you become distracted? I love you deeply and am calling you close to My heart in this hour, for when you make Me the center of all things in your life, you will know peace and fulfillment. It all comes from Me. I am grooming you as My beautiful Bride, but the Bride makes herself ready. She is not engaged in the distractions of the world or the enticements of the flesh. My Bride is smitten by My love and responds. My Bride has one prima-ry, undistracted affection—Me. When she arises, I am on her mind and she seeks Me. Throughout her day, I am foremost in her thoughts, and at night when she lays to rest, I am her final meditation. My Bride is always filled with fresh oil and does not neglect the most important part of her life—Me.

What can worldly possessions offer you? Only fading pleasure. What can man's efforts produce? Only temporary satisfaction. What can money buy? Only things that rust and moth destroy and thieves break in and steal (see Matt. 6:19). Why do you focus on things that do not satisfy? Why are you distracted?

The enemy has launched an assault of distraction upon My people in order to hinder them from coming to Me, but in this hour My Spirit will call My people back into divine order, keeping Me as their central focus in all things. They will return to Me in response to My love. A fresh and deepened revelation of My love will be granted them so that they will return—they will come.

A company of believers will be raised up in this hour whose passion is completely Mine. They will know Me and desire nothing but Me. They will love Me because they understand and know through experience the love I have for them. They will seek Me all their days without giving in to distraction, and I will fill them and bless them. Their love for Me will cause them to focus without effort.

There will also be many who will realize that their hearts are far from Me and they will return to their first love in fasting and prayer. They will cry out for grace to return for they are dissatisfied. I will answer them and grant them the desires of their heart. Once again, they will love Me and serve Me with undistracted focus.

Ministries will emerge in this era to teach, mentor, and train My people to love Me with all their hearts. I will be the focus of these ministries. Even though they will teach life skills, spiritual gifts, and biblical principles, and be committed to the great commission, their main focus is Me—Jesus! Their message will carry one theme: Me—Jesus. Many of these ministries will be led by younger-generation leaders who only want Me. They do not long for title, attention, possessions, or promotion—they simply long for Me. They will be humble before Me and truly embrace the cross, taking it up daily as they follow Me.

Many will tell them, "Lighten up—you are too intense! You are too radical! People need more than just Jesus—your life needs more than just Jesus." But they will follow Me in fullness of focus, in purity of heart, and in outrageous love, for they know My love and have received My love. They will not be distracted. As a result of these Jesus-focused believers, I will emerge in the earth to be seen by the masses, for they will not simply present programs, teachings, and events to attract people—they will present *Me*. I will be the focus and they will hide themselves in Me.

Many leaders in this era will dismantle the very things in their ministries that bring distraction. I will lead them to simplify so that their attention will not be absorbed by the mundane. The shackles of distraction will fall from them and they will once again gaze upon Me and seek My face. They will be renewed in their faith and I will increase their effectiveness for they will be led by My Spirit. They will return to prayer, worship, and the study of the Word and will be free again to obey My leading in simple faith. This is how I obeyed My Father's leading when I walked on the earth. The very things I saw My Father do, I did. The things I heard Him say, I spoke. I walked in close relationship with Him, obeying His voice and following His lead. I did not allow meaningless distractions to take My focus.

Many will come to Me in this era. Many will follow Me. Many will serve Me well—for I am their focus.

INSIGHTS

Life is full of distractions, but there is only one thing that is important. We see this in the story of Martha and Mary of Bethany:

> *Now it happened as they went that He entered a certain village; and a certain woman named Martha welcomed Him into her house. And she had a sister called Mary, who also sat at Jesus' feet and heard His word. But Martha was* **distracted** *with much serving, and she approached Him and said, "Lord, do You not care that my sister has left me to serve alone? Therefore tell her to help me." And Jesus answered and said to her, "Martha, Martha, you are worried and troubled about many things. But* **one thing is needed***, and Mary has chosen that good part, which will not be taken away from her"* (Luke 10:38-42 NKJV).

When Martha met Jesus, she had a heart to serve Him and welcomed Him into her family home. Her sister Mary was present also, and Mary appears to have immediately positioned herself at the feet of Jesus, hearing His Word. I can clearly imagine the scenario: Mary was totally captured by Jesus and engaged in His very presence with nothing distracting her while Martha was agitated because her sister wasn't helping with the meal prep or performing the outward tasks at hand.

When Martha brought up the subject to Jesus, inviting Him to set Mary straight, His answer was not what she expected: *"Martha, Martha, you are worried and troubled about many things. But one thing is needed, and Mary has chosen that good part, which will not be taken away from her."*

That was probably a very hard thing for Martha to hear, but it was necessary. Martha had a good heart and desired Jesus to be in the midst of her household. She also wanted to serve Him well, but she didn't realize the most important thing: being positioned in His presence to receive the Word that comes forth from His mouth—the Word that you can only receive while your attention is completely fixed on Him.

Jesus was Mary's focus while Martha's focus was accomplishing all the tasks needed to serve Him well. There is nothing wrong with engaging in tasks, but there needs to be right order and perspective. Jesus is first. When our focus is upon Him, then it is carried into the tasks and assignments at hand. When Jesus is first in our affections, He fills everything else with His grace, love, wisdom, and presence.

I love, the song "Jesus at the Center" by Adam Ranney, Israel Houghton, and Micah Massey.

> Jesus be the center of my life
> Jesus be the center of my life
> From beginning to the end
> It will always be, it's always been You
> Jesus, Jesus
> Nothing else matters
> Nothing in this world will do
> 'Cause Jesus You're the center
> Everything revolves around You
> Jesus

Some of you reading this chapter might feel conflicted because your heart wants to focus on Jesus, but you find yourself constantly giving in to distraction. Paul describes this battle in the Book of Romans:

> *For I delight in the law of God according to the inward man. But I see another law in my members, warring against the law of my mind, and bringing me into captivity* (Romans 7:22-23 NKJV).

He goes on to teach us that it is Jesus Christ Himself who sets us free from this conflict and:

> *There is therefore now no condemnation to those who are in Christ Jesus, who do not walk according to the flesh, but according to the Spirit. For the law of the Spirit of life in Christ Jesus has made me free from the law of sin and death* (Romans 8:1-2 NKJV).

You do not need to walk in condemnation, fear, or shame when you are distracted; you simply need to turn away from the distraction and look to Jesus. He knows your heart's deepest desires and will fulfill them. You might be wondering how you could possibly keep your mind centered on Jesus every moment of every day. Being focused on Jesus relates more to your heart's position and passion rather than moment-by-moment mental focus and acknowledgment, but when you grow in your focus you will also grow in precious grace to have Jesus become everything to you in every part of your day and in all you do.

Here are some principles that might help you walk free from distractions and engage in a new level of consecrated focus in the Lord.

REFOCUS MOMENTS

Evaluate

The first question to ask is, "Am I distracted or am I fully focused? Is Jesus the center of my life?" There will probably be evaluation on various levels, but be as honest as you can.

Invite Jesus to Help You

Jesus will surely help you and give you the answer to your desire to have Him positioned at the very center of your life without distraction. He will not withhold that from you. Pray in faith for Jesus to help you focus and make Him the center of your life with a full restoration of first love—pray without wavering in unbelief or doubt. When you pray according to His will, He hears you and grants you your request (see 1 John 5:14-15). This is His will for you so you can be confident.

KNOW YOU'RE HIS = CONFIDENT
PRESENT YOURSELF BOLDLY BEFORE HIM
ASK, AGREEING WITH HIS WILL
HE WILL HEAR,
WE WILL OBTAIN.

Refocus Moments

When you find yourself losing focus, invite the Holy Spirit to move your focus back to Jesus. You will be able to think on Him immediately then. You can engage in refocus moments throughout your day. It only takes a minute or more. Some people call these moments "personal retreats." When you focus on Him in that exercise, engage with Him from your heart. Praise Him or converse with Him—simply acknowledge Him and your desire to make Him number one in your life.

Discipline

Often Christians do not like the word *discipline*, but it is a healthy practice. We don't mind being told to discipline ourselves in diet, exercise, or training for something we enjoy or for a career advantage, but somehow, when it is mentioned in the context of our devotional and spiritual walk, it is called "religious" and we run far from it.

The word *discipline* comes from the word *disciple*. In regard to discipline, the apostle Paul said:

> *But I discipline my body and bring it into subjection, lest, when I have preached to others, I myself should become disqualified* (1 Corinthians 9:27 NKJV).

The writer of Hebrews adds:

> *All discipline for the moment seems not to be joyful, but sorrowful; yet to those who have been trained by it, afterwards it yields* the peaceful fruit of righteousness (Hebrews 12:11).

RIGHT STANDING WITH GOD

Some suggested disciplines might include daily scheduled:

- Bible reading
- Prayer time
- Worship
- Praying in tongues
- Journaling

We don't discipline ourselves to obtain favor with God. We are already favored by Him when we receive Christ as our Savior. Neither do we discipline ourselves in order to warrant salvation, for it is a gift. However, we can use spiritual disciplines to create focus on Jesus, and the focus creates growth in relationship with the Lord as we are positioned to receive from Him and to lavish Him with our love.

TO MINISTER TO HIM

Disciplined practice is usually always the element that brings success in natural things, and yet we so often negate its value in our spiritual life. If you look at the life of any successful or accomplished athlete, artist, musician, author, or business person, you will find disciplined practice is one of the foundation stones of their success.

Let's practice leaning into the presence of Jesus. Let's practice pursuing Him until He is fully our focus. *PRACTICING THE PRESENCE*

Thoughts to Ponder

How would you evaluate your focus level on Jesus?

Do you hunger to love Him more?

Imagine your life fully surrendered to Jesus. What would look different than now?

What benefits come as a result of being fully focused on Jesus?

What will it cost you to become fully focused? Are you willing to pay the price?

PRAYER FOR FOCUSING ON JESUS

Heavenly Father,

Forgive me for the many distractions I have allowed in my life that keep me from being fully focused on Jesus as my first love. I choose to return to my first love and ask You to pour out great enabling grace upon me. Deepen the revelation of Your love for me and grant me fresh encounters. I love You because You first loved me—help me to fully realize Your love for me so that I might respond in fullness. Grant me the desires of my heart.

In Jesus' name I pray,

Amen.

Chapter Three

AN ERA OF REFORMATION

*See, I have this day set thee over the nations and over
the kingdoms, to root out, and to pull down, and to
destroy, and to throw down, to build, and to plant.*
—JEREMIAH 1:10 KJV

Prophecy

I AM a God of order and justice and not a God of confusion or unrighteousness. You will see a shift in this season marking a new era that will separate good from evil and evil from good. In the previous season I poured out rivers of divine refreshment from My throne and invited My people to freely enjoy the current of My goodness and glory. I opened up the wells of My mercy, grace, and unconditional love and invited My people to imbibe deeply. I held nothing back.

Many came to know Me in deep and intimate ways and have followed Me faithfully, yet others who encountered and experienced My kindness have failed to embrace My ways and have corrupted many through their waywardness, complacency, and tolerance. It is time to beckon all to return to My righteous and uncompromised order.

As the church goes, so go the nations. Many nations are in disarray because My church is in disarray, but this will change for I am calling for reformation and divine alignment.

It is time to reform. It is time to align. It is time to awaken My people unto My truth. My church will experience shakings and I will purge and reform it; My church will look different in the days to come, for this is not a season of "business as usual." Reformation in the church and reformation through the church will be established in this era.

It is time for My righteous reformers who are in true partnership with Me to arise and call for alignment to My Word and ways. My reformers will carry great authority and will initiate change that will bring transformation. They will address things that need to be uprooted and destroyed and they will also build and plant.

Due to their bold and uncompromised stand, My reformers will be misunderstood and persecuted by many in My church as well as in the world, but they will represent My interests alone and not the interests of those who have rebelled against My Word. They will open up their mouths wide and I will fill them. They will not have regard for their own lives even though the cost might be great. They will be marked by love, and you will know them by My love as

28

love will be their motive and greatest aim—love will fill their hearts. They will love Me, they will love My church, and they will love the cause that I burn within their hearts.

Many of those I am marking as reformers are not yet known, for they have been hidden for such a time as this. They have been fasting and praying. They have been seeking My face. They have been preparing their hearts before Me and have embraced My discipline. They have humbled themselves before Me and have submitted to My dealings in their lives. They are ready to arise.

My reformers will lift their voices with bold faith in this hour and will not be silent. I will speak to them in the night hours and I will speak to them at noonday. They will know My voice and they will be fearless and of good courage. My reformers will not only deliver the message, they will become the message that will reform. My reformers are true servants wearing mantles of prophets, priests, and kings.

My company of reformers are not interested in being popular in man's eyes; rather, they are committed to pleasing their Father in Heaven. They are not interested in money, fame, or personal gain. My reformers will raise the bar and fearlessly and lovingly confront lawlessness, injustice, and those things that need alignment to My Word.

Watch and see what I will do, says the Lord. This is an era of tensions that will bring about alignment through shakings and breakings. Much alignment is needed. Pray for reformation!

REFORMATION
RE-FORMING
SETTING ON THE RIGHT PATH

INSIGHTS

There is a difference between reformation and revival. While revival speaks of renewal, refreshment, and that which brings life back to what is dead or listless, reformation involves causing things to improve by making corrections, removing any faults, remaking, and implementing change; changing a person's behavior; or rebuilding the structure of something.

Reformation

The Protestant Reformation was a movement within the 16th century, issuing a challenge to the Roman Catholic Church and its sovereign papal authority. It posed a religious, political, intellectual, and cultural upheaval that divided and weakened Catholic Europe, setting in place the structures and beliefs that would define the continent in the modern era.

Martin Luther, a key reformer, while engaged in service as a monk in the Catholic Church, was burdened by the oppressive religious and non-biblical structures that hindered people from receiving salvation and knowing God personally. In 1517 he published the famous "Ninety-five Theses," including the famous biblical claim, *"the just shall live by faith"* (Rom. 1:17 NKJV).

The key ideas of the Protestant Reformation included a call to purify the church and a belief that the Bible, not tradition, should be the sole source of spiritual authority. Luther and other reformers challenged the Catholic Church's ability to define Christian practice and contended for religious and political power to be redistributed from sovereign papal authority to Bible-believing pastors and princes. It caused opposition amongst the religious leaders, and by 1521 the

Edict of Worms condemned Luther and officially banned citizens of the Roman Empire from defending or promoting his beliefs.

The challenge triggered wars, persecutions, and the "Counter-Reformation," which was the Catholic Church's delayed but forceful response to the Protestants. In 1555 the treaty, "Peace of Augsburg," allowed for the coexistence of Catholicism and Lutheranism in Germany. The "Peace of Westphalia," which followed, was a series of peace treaties signed between May and October 1648, largely ending the European wars of religion. Protestantism was free to grow as a result.

Luther and the other reformers were the first to skillfully use the power of the printing press to give their ideas a wide audience. They brought about historical religious, cultural, intellectual, and political reform based on biblical truth as they fearlessly contended to usher in a new era.

Using the Protestant Reformation as an example, you can see that reformation involves much confrontation, opposition, resistance, and battle. Reform also takes time. Much grace is needed to serve God's purposes in reformation, and seasons of reform are sobering times.

Other amazing examples of reformation in history can be seen in the historical First and Second Great Awakenings (1730s–1870s). In the United States, biblical foundations were laid in the nation, a strong call to repentance was issued, and social injustices were addressed, fought for, and established through this period of reformation.

One particular area of reform in that season was the abolition of slavery. In the 17th century, English Quakers and some Evangelical denominations condemned slavery as un-Christian. Abolition was part of the message of the First Great Awakening of the 1730s and

1740s. In Britain in the 1790s–1830s, William Wilberforce, Thornton, and other reformers formed the Clapham Sect—a group of Church of England social reformers based in Clapham, London. They were prominent, wealthy Anglicans. One of their commonly held political and social views was the liberation of slaves.

It took many decades of work, both in British society and in Parliament, but these reformers eventually were rewarded when the Slave Trade Act finally passed in 1807, banning the practice of buying and selling slaves throughout the British Empire. After further years of campaigning, the Slavery Abolition Act was passed in 1833, finally freeing all British slaves.

Believers in America under the conviction of the Holy Spirit during the Second Great Awakening (1790–1870) became influential voices and forces in the reform. As a result of both voice and action, many political debates, societal eruptions, and polarized resistance, the United States federal government criminalized the international slave trade in 1808 and made slavery unconstitutional in 1865 as a result of the Civil War.

As you can clearly see in both the Protestant Reformation and the First and Second Great Awakenings, reform was needed in the areas that were addressed in those days. We are enjoying important freedoms today due to reformation. Where would we be without these reforms? We would be living in a very different world.

Revival

Revival speaks of refreshing, renewal, and revitalization and can manifest in various forms and measures. We will always welcome both personal and corporate revival. Revival is like a shower that brings refreshment, but revival does not always bring reform.

There have been many historical revivals throughout church history and each of them is unique. One modern-day example is noted in 1994, when a powerful move of the Spirit broke out in Toronto, Canada. Many credible Christian leaders called it a true renewal or revival. The intensity of the Spirit graced the nightly meetings that were hosted six nights per week for many years and subsequently spread to the nations for over two decades with unusual signs and wonders. I had the honor of frequently visiting those gatherings during the initial years of the outpouring and my life and ministry was greatly refreshed and changed as a result. The masses who gathered nightly from all over the world were powerfully touched and many were changed and empowered for Kingdom ministry.

Often ministers testified publicly to thousands of how prior to being personally revived by God's Spirit in the meetings, they were ready to leave their ministries and callings as they were disillusioned, tired, battle-worn, and without fresh vision. However, one single encounter in the Lord's undeniable presence changed everything for them. They were revitalized, empowered, blessed, and filled with an awareness of God's refreshing love and with new mandates. It was a glorious season for the church worldwide, and although some resisted and persecuted the outpouring, those who were touched by it couldn't help but spread the good news of what God was doing. Believers gathered from the nations nightly in Toronto, and when they returned the Spirit was poured out in like manner in their communities and nations. It was an unstoppable fresh wind.

One of the predominant messages in that renewal was to know the love of the Father. Many were deeply touched, healed, and delivered as they received the revelation of the unconditional love of Father God. His mercy and grace filled them, freeing them to serve Him with all their hearts. Two of the predominant "signs" were what was referred to as "holy laughter" and "drunkenness" in the Holy Spirit, similar to what you read about in Acts 2 at Pentecost. It was as though God was throwing a party of celebration with all the trimmings for His dear children.

I heard many prophecies during that time declare that God was revealing His extravagant love and filling His people with the new wine of His joy so they would be ready for the treacherous days to come.

Many believers were being personally refreshed and revived, but the temperature of society was left unchanged for the most part. At the same time, liberal mindsets and immorality escalated in the world and demonic reforms were in full motion. In some nations that were originally founded on Christian principles, laws were put into place condoning late-term abortions, same-sex marriage, and legalization of marijuana. Sexual promiscuity became normalized; the pressure to accept transgender lifestyles increased; pornographic addictions and sex trafficking became epidemic, putting masses of children at risk; and our youth were plagued with opioid and alcohol dependencies that took the lives of many. Not only was the entertainment industry and media propagating many of these anti-biblical values, governments were passing laws and the education system was filling our youth with brainwashing distortions.

While the world was escalating in anti-biblical values, for the most part the church remained silent, although there was a powerful remnant of amazing believers with radical faith who trumpeted the Lord's Word, gathered and activated the intercessors, and put feet on the ground. Unfortunately, however, there were sections of the church that became compromised and embraced these worldly and anti-biblical mindsets. A few denominations supported same-sex marriage, and increased numbers of believers and church leaders without conscience violated New Testament moral conduct by imbibing in or tolerating and excusing sexual sin, drunkenness, pornography, and false doctrines such as universalism and other New Age practices. These ones often called those who confronted such conduct legalistic and religious. Deception filled many, calling good evil and evil good.

When the scales of injustice and sin weigh heavy, reformation is needed. Confrontation is needed. Repentance is needed. God's desire is to see heavenly glory manifest in the earth. Heaven's atmosphere is holy. In order to see change we need *"to root out, and to pull down, and to destroy, and to throw down, to build, and to plant"* (Jer. 1:10 KJV).

Reform in society will come when the church is aligned. A reformation will come to the church in this new era that will uproot false beliefs and deceptive and sinful practices. The Lord will lead His people, calling us to raise our voice and take action. Let the reformation begin—in me, in you, in us.

Thoughts to Ponder

Do you believe reformation is needed in this era? If so, why?

What areas of reform are needed in today's society? In the church?

Dream big with God about reformation in your nation. What does it look like?

Do you need personal revival? If so, in what areas?

Do you need personal reformation? What needs to be rooted out and what needs to be planted?

PRAYER FOR REFORMATION

Heavenly Father,

I long to see reformation in my life, in my family, city, region, and nation. Have Your way in me. I invite Your Spirit to fill me with fresh insight and revelation on what needs to be uprooted, adjusted, and aligned in my life. Align me completely to Your purposes and allow me to be used by You to bring reformation.

I receive by faith in the name of Jesus,

Amen.

Chapter *Four*

AN ERA OF EXPOSURE

*Do not participate in the unfruitful deeds of
darkness, but instead even* expose them*... But all
things become visible when they are exposed by the
light, for everything that becomes visible is light.*
—EPHESIANS 5:11,13

THERE IS NOTHING CONCEALED
THAT WILL NOT BE ~~MADE KNOWN~~ DISCLOSED
OR HIDDEN THAT WILL NOT BE
MADE KNOWN. **Prophecy** (NIV)

Everything hidden and covered up will soon be
exposed. For the facade is falling down, and nothing
will be kept secret for long. Whatever you have spoken
in private will be public knowledge, and what you have
whispered secretly behind closed doors will be broadcast far and wide for all to hear (Luke 12:2-3 TPT).

I am Light, says the Lord, and in Me there is no darkness at all. I will shine My light into the darkness of men's hearts and ways and expose things that have not been seen or noticed by others. Shock waves will hit My Body as deeds of darkness become exposed.

I have watched My people fall into diverse temptations even though I was there to beckon them to turn away. After they partook of the temptation, I reached out by knocking with conviction on the door of their heart over and over. When they continued to ignore My conviction and invitation to repent, I sent others to give warning and to call them back into alignment with Me and My truth. But they failed to listen. They failed to repent. So, I again persisted by sending even others, but still to no avail. It is now time to openly expose.

Some have been engaged in deeds of darkness behind closed doors for many years, but even as I took My servant Ezekiel into the inner part of the temple and revealed to him the abominations that were taking place in secret, so also in this hour will I make these things known.

My heart is to love and to heal. Do you not know that whatever a man sows he will also reap? Do you not know that if you sow to the flesh, you will reap corruption? I love My people and I love all whom I have created, but I must rescue. I must deliver. I have given time to repent, but those who have hardened their hearts have refused to turn away from the deeds of darkness. I have called, but many have not listened. They have ignored My beckoning call. The darkness is spreading and infecting others around them like

38

a virus and it must be stopped. My people must be clean and free; therefore, I must act. Many will say, "Why does this need to be exposed?" I will answer, "Because this is love."

Without exposure, healing cannot come. Without exposure, cleansing cannot come. Without exposure, alignment cannot come. Without exposure, solutions cannot come. It is time. My house shall be cleansed. Even as I cleansed My house by exposing and overturning the money changers' tables, so also shall I cleanse My house in this hour. I will shine My light and expose the deeds of darkness so that true freedom and Kingdom life will be made manifest.

TURN THE TABLES!

Hidden Agendas in the World

In this era there will be an exposure of evil hidden agendas, especially in areas of government, business, science, media, and the medical field. The love of money and the lust for power and position have put many in jeopardy due to the hidden agendas of evil men and women. Exposure will come and cause that which they have deceptively built to weaken due to public exposure.

Trust Levels Will Be Challenged

Due to the exposure, many will be tempted to lose trust and some individuals will even lose their faith. This is an hour to walk closely with Me, for I never compromise what is right and I never change. I am the same yesterday, today, and forever. I always walk in integrity, love, truth, and wisdom. Even when men and women shall fail you, I will not fail you. Draw close to Me in this hour. Trust Me. *SEEK ME!*

Hidden Gifts, Talents, and Callings Will Be Exposed

Not only will I be exposing the very things that bring harm to My people in order for healing, cleansing, and deliverance to come, I will also expose hidden gifts, talents, and callings within the lives of My people. In this era, many will suddenly become aware of deposits of My Spirit that have been lying dormant and unseen within them. Even those who are close to them will be amazed when they see their loved ones arise into sudden visibility. *!!!!*

I will raise up many prophets who will have eyes to see the hidden potential, gifts, and callings in My people and will call them to arise in boldness to fulfill their callings. */* Some who have been hidden for many years will come into visibility in this era, for they have been seasoned in the secret place. *THE SECRET PLACE OF THE MOST HIGH, THE SHADOW OF THE ALMIGHTY*

This era is an era of exposure: an exposure of sin, deception, evil agendas, and also of hidden gifts, talents, and callings.

INSIGHTS

Most often, you cannot fix a problem unless you clearly identify it. I remember when I was sixteen years of age, I began to have flu symptoms in my last class of the day. I felt slightly warm, had a faint headache and nausea, and my abdomen was slightly tender. I walked home and the symptoms intensified. I went to my room immediately and curled up on my bed as the abdominal pain increased. When my parents came home from work late that day, they realized something was wrong. It was unusual to find their daughter in bed that early, but they also came to realize that the symptoms, although not severe, should be checked out. They called the doctor and he instructed them to take me to the emergency ward of the hospital immediately.

In the hospital the doctor examined me and performed lab tests to expose the problem and confirm his suspicions. The blood tests along with his physical exam exposed the culprit—an inflamed appendix. The exposure was not the solution and it would have been a fatal mistake for him to send me home or to leave me untreated following the exposure. The exposure only served to create an opportunity to implement the solution. Within hours I was in the operating room, having my appendix surgically removed. The doctor explained to our family following the surgery that the appendix was ready to burst. It was extremely inflamed and if we had waited even another hour, I could have possibly even lost my life.

I woke up from surgery in a lot of pain and I remember thinking that the cure seemed more painful than the cause. It took me a few weeks to heal up completely, but then I enjoyed optimum health. Even though the recovery was initially painful, if I had not had the surgery I would not be writing this book today. The exposure was vital—it saved my life.

Whistle-Blowers

Exposure of things that are harmful to you or others—although painful, uncomfortable, and confusing at times in the midst of the process—will help to bring healing and safety for others in the future.

Exposure makes way for alignment. I remember a time when the Lord called me to be part of a team to serve in the exposing of some abusive behaviors in the life of a Christian minister. The minister had been using his authority to lure young women and men into sexual encounters—a number of them were his interns. He personally abused alcohol and drugs, used foul language, communicated unclean jokes, and was sexually addicted. He also endorsed, facilitated, and invited others to partake of these vices. Many of these behaviors had been addressed by his overseers on a few occasions over a fifteen- to twenty-year period in addition to other sins. During these times of non-public confrontation he appeared to be sorrowful, but there was no true repentance and as a result the behaviors escalated behind the scenes.

Finally, victims of his behavior and vices came to those outside of his "core team" to share what was happening behind closed doors. When individuals representing the reports of the victims confronted him, he denied it. When they went to his overseer, they were refused a meeting. As a result of the resistance to give attention to the allegations, a whistle-blower took it to social media on behalf of the victims. Due to that exposure, it could no longer be swept under the carpet or hidden in back-room confrontations. An outside, objective investigation was launched, and dozens more victims came forward to share tragic incidences of abuse. An official report was prepared that also offered the offender an opportunity to address the issues and share his heart (unfortunately, he declined the opportunity). A panel of seasoned, objective, and respected ministers reviewed the reports and made a final and public evaluation that this man did not meet the biblical character qualifications for ministry and, without mentioning specific cases, supported the allegations.

The team of whistle-blowers who represented the voice of the victims paid a huge price. During the investigation process, the perpetrator of these behaviors (and his team) kicked back with violent, accusative verbal attacks and threats toward those bringing the exposure. Initially, the perpetrator denied the allegations; although over time he changed his story to accept most of the items in a general sense while excusing the behavior as that which was "repented of" and "under the blood" even though a number of the allegations were very current—even right up to the time of the investigation.

Due to the public exposure, there was so much pain on everyone's part—the victims for sure, the perpetrator and his family, the whistle-blowers, and the general body of Christ who were watching it all unfold. I remember in the beginning of it all not wanting to be involved and definitely not wanting it to go public, but the Lord spoke to me as well as many other prophets, saying that it had to go public as God Himself was exposing it so that the enemy's grip would be weakened and captives would go free. The following scripture was given to me by the Spirit in the beginning of the season, and it often haunted me due to the weight of this assignment:

> *Everything hidden and covered up will soon be exposed. For the facade is falling down, and nothing will be kept secret for long. Whatever you have spoken in private will be public knowledge, and what you have whispered secretly behind closed doors will be broadcast far and wide for all to hear* (Luke 12:2-3 TPT).

There is a difference between an individual who has fallen into a temptation, repents, and receives cleansing, and the one who willfully continues in sin. And there is a difference between one who harms himself/herself and one who has predatory behavior, intentionally grooming vulnerable individuals to serve their purposes.

God is calling His whistle-blowers in this hour, but beware! He always will desire to deal with sin privately first, for He truly loves those overcome by sin, but He hates the sin—sin hurts people. That is why He sends His Holy Spirit to convict over and over again. He is so patient. If there is no successful response, then He will reveal it to others. Everything must be done to help one who is struggling; but also, if there are victims involved, they must not be forgotten but protected. They must be tended to and cared for. Going public is a very last resort and it must be done with care. First of all, that which is being reported must be accurate. "Thou shalt not bear false witness." The accounts shared must be true and accurate. In addition, there can be no natural anger, offense, or bitterness involved. *"The anger of man does not achieve the righteousness of God"* (James 1:20). Everything must be weighed carefully according to the wisdom of God, and there must be *love*. Love for the offender and love for the victims. Love for all involved. Love can be tough, but it always seeks the highest good for the sake of others—all others. When God exposes, it is in love and for the sake of love because He *is* love.

Exposure will raise the bar, but it will also reveal hearts. Some, in the name of mercy, would like to cover up and make excuses for harmful behavior, blindly releasing perpetrators to continue while denying care for the victims and scriptural instruction regarding the sin and behaviors. (While "love covers" it does not "cover up.") Others would like to see the sinner and the sin confronted in love and truth, that there be full repentance along with restitution, while healing for all (including the offender, the victims, and those that are involved indirectly) is a priority. Exposure reveals which side of the line people will live on. Exposure reveals hearts, intents, and positions.

Good News About Exposure

Although the exposure of hidden sin is disheartening and troubling for sure, when properly walked through it will bring about good in the end. It will raise the bar and bring alignment. But there is more good news. The same Holy Spirit who exposes sin is also the one who exposes the goodness in each of us—our gifts, talents, and abilities.

In this season, the Holy Spirit will reveal things within us that will delightfully shock us! He will also bring revelation and exposure to plans and purposes that have been hidden until this time. There are many wonderful surprises to be unfolded in this next era. Get positioned for the greatest exposure ever of God's purposes and destiny.

Thoughts to Ponder

Would you like the Holy Spirit to expose in you anything that needs to come into alignment with His Word?

If not, why not?

If so, invite Him now to reveal to you anything that He desires to make known to you. He will.

Why would a God of Love desire to expose harmful things in us or others?

Why is exposure needed in this hour?

PRAYER FOR EXPOSURE

Heavenly Father,

I trust Your love. Expose in me anything that needs to be brought into the light and empower me to repent fully and make things right with anyone I have hurt or harmed.

Help me also to see all Your wonderful attributes in my life.

Expose Your purposes in me and fulfill them.

In Jesus' name I pray,

Amen.

Chapter *Five*

AN ERA OF SOLUTIONS

Truly I say to you, whoever says to this mountain,
"Be taken up and cast into the sea," and does not
doubt in his heart, but believes that what he says
is going to happen, it will be granted him.
—MARK 11:23

Prophecy

For every problem I have a solution, says the Lord. I am the God of all wisdom and I am your Creator. Many have looked at the obstacles before them and have been overwhelmed. They have lost sight of who I am and have seen the problem they are facing to be greater and larger than My ability to conquer. Is there anything too hard for Me?

In this coming era, you will see mountains and obstacles move in your personal lives and even on national and international levels, for I am a God of solutions. When I delivered My people out of Egypt, did I not bring solutions to every problem? When they looked at the Red Sea in front of them while the armies of Egypt attacked from behind, they could not see the solution, but I saw the solution. It was easy. I simply rolled back the sea and directed My people to the other side. When they were safe, I swallowed up the pursuing army in the sea. The horse and rider were thrown into the sea, but My people were safe. I was their solution.

When they longed for food but did not know where to find it as there was none in sight—they could see a dry, desolate desert before them—I became their food. I opened up the heavens and poured out fresh manna upon the ground every day for them and they ate until they were fully satisfied.

They never lacked because I was their solution when it looked like there was no natural solution in sight. When they were thirsty and there was not a drop of water to be found, they became anxious and murmured. They thought for sure they would surely perish, for they could not see the solution. Once again, I was their solution and brought forth water from the rock for them and their thirst was quenched. They never lacked water in the wilderness because I was their solution.

In this coming era there will be many problems and obstacles that will require solutions. Remember that there is nothing too difficult for Me. I am the one who will grant solutions, and many of these solutions will be noted in history. You will see solutions given to My servants in government that will resolve problems in society. In the natural, many might say, "This solution will not work," but when I am giving solutions they will succeed, for My solutions are supernatural.

In this era, you will learn to speak to the mountains that stand before you and they will surely move for you because you will not doubt in your heart that My power is enough. You will believe and things will shift. Do not limit in your mind what I am able to do. Do not say, "Oh, but this problem is too big!" I tell you, I AM the God of solutions. I am the God who is able to work everything together for good to those who love Me and who are called according to My purpose (see Rom. 8:28).

Are you facing problems where you lack faith in seeing them solved? Look up. I am the God of solutions, and as you look to Me and worship Me you will see things shift. Believe. Expect. Solutions are on their way.

INSIGHTS

Every problem has a solution. The greatest problem ever was when mankind sinned against God in the garden, causing everyone to be infected with sin in their DNA and for corruption to fill the earth. This was a horrific problem because the sin separated us from God with no way for us to make the wrong right, and everything became subject to destruction, decay, and death; but God had the solution prepared. He sent His own Son to be the sacrifice for our sins and in exchange gave us His righteousness (right standing with God).

He made a plan for everything to be redeemed. This is all available to everyone who believes. If God can reconcile sinful mankind to Himself, then there is nothing He cannot do.

In the last chapter I shared a story about an experience I had been involved with, exposing the sins of a Christian leader. My heart broke for the minister, but I was especially burdened for the victims. It was a difficult season as I listened to story after story. Their pain was deep. They were told by the minister not to speak or to share regarding their encounters together but to keep it a secret. The victims were confused, ashamed, and began to blame themselves. They were alone and did not know how to move on. A few of them even lost their faith in God and others became addicted to drugs or alcohol to numb the pain.

When the final and official statement was made regarding the guilt of the minister, I was very sad and struggled deeply. Everything was exposed but the victims were still hurting without help or aid, and the minister was moving on. Nothing really changed except for the fact that the exposure was now public. I was weeping over it, feeling overwhelmed, when the Spirit of God said, "Do not weep, for I am the God of solutions." Suddenly, what I would call a "heavenly download" filled me. It was a strategy that would help the victims—it was a solution for their devastation, loneliness, and despair. It came like a blueprint, so to speak, containing a solution to help. I perceived the whole solution in a moment of time. Within the next few days, our ministry birthed Voice4Victims. We then developed the entire department with Facebook, websites, resources, and a full start-up team. In God's solution plan we had been given a four-fold mandate that included:

Mission Statement

To offer help, support, encouragement, and voice to victims of sexual, spiritual, domestic, and physical abuse in the church.

4-Fold Purpose

1. Help

- **Helpline**: Many victims do not know to whom to reach out. They have lost trust and have never been able to tell their story or to share their pain. Through the email **helpline**, help@voice4victims .life, victims will be able to reach out in confidentiality to a seasoned support team.

- **Public Social Media**: We will utilize a public Facebook (facebook.com/voice4victims.life) forum as well as Instagram (@voice4victims) to help reach those who need help.

- **Intercession**: A team of skilled intercessors are assigned to pray for those who are victims and will also cover individual requests.

- **Testimony**: Testimonies are powerful and will be posted to encourage victims and to build faith and hope.

2. Support

- **Prayer Ministry**: Teams of non-professional but trained prayer ministers are available to help victims find freedom in Christ. Resources and referrals for inner healing and deliverance will also be available.

- **Professional Counselors, Therapists, Social Workers**: A networked team of professional counselors, therapists, and social workers is available to give direction and help.

3. Legal Team

- Often the abuse suffered by victims is criminal. A legal team of investigators and attorneys will be available to give insight on how to move forward.

- Frequently asked questions will be posted on the site to help victims understand legal processes.

4. Resources

- Valuable resources will be recommended that will aid in the healing and education of victims as well as preventative information through articles, blogs, media, training events, books, and network information with other organizations.

Almost immediately, we began to have victims of abuse in the church contact us, sharing their stories. Training modules for prayer teams were built, resources were collected, social media posts were being created, and the solution was at work.

Some have asked, "Why didn't you call the department Voice4Survivors or Voice4Victors?" They believed that using the word *victim* was keeping the abused in a victim mindset. Although I understand their concern, in this case it actually did the opposite. Healing couldn't come until the victims were able to embrace the fact that they had been violated. Until that time, many did not feel worthy to share or to get help—they lived in their shame and remorse. They were confused because, after all, "This was an 'anointed leader'—a 'man of God' who led me into this." Even though their leader had targeted them, groomed them, and used his authority to lure them into acts that they were not comfortable with, they were made to believe that because they were giving in to his authority, they were "consenting" and had no right to share it with anyone. Once they took ownership of what happened to them, they began to find freedom. If they didn't identify with being victimized first, they wouldn't be able to find their victory. Exposure has to come before the solution. They surely now have the opportunity to go from *victim* to *victor.*

I believe that in this next era we will see many solutions. Out of some of the most painful situations will come glorious solutions. You might even be facing some things right now that look impossible, *but* the God of solutions is at work and is willing to grant you access to a solution so glorious that it will cause praise to explode in you. Let expectation arise. It's going to be a great era!

Thoughts to Ponder

Do you have something in your life right now that could use a solution? What is it?

Do you believe that God can give you a solution and move the "mountain" out of your way?

Are there things in society you see that need a solution? What are they?

Do you believe that change can come to this situation if God grants a solution?

Dream big and see in your imagination that problem and others fully solved. What does it look like?

PRAYER FOR SOLUTION

Heavenly Father,

Help my faith to grow so I can believe You to be my solution in every situation I face. I glorify and exalt You as my solution.

May my heart be open to receive Your wisdom and instruction that bring forth victory in every situation I encounter.

In Jesus' name I pray,

Amen.

Chapter *Six*

An Era of the Plumb Line

*For the word of God is living and active and full
of power [making it operative, energizing, and
effective]. It is sharper than any two-edged sword,
penetrating as far as the division of the soul and spirit
[the completeness of a person], and of both joints and
marrow [the deepest parts of our nature], exposing and
judging the very thoughts and intentions of the heart.*
—Hebrews 4:12 AMP

Prophecy

In the month of December 2019, I was in a powerful prayer meeting where I saw a vivid vision of a large glistening sword coming down from heaven piercing into the earth. I heard the Lord say, "This is My plumb line. It is the Sword of Truth." I saw that it was a sharp, two-edged sword. I then heard the Spirit say, "The two edges you see on the sword are My kindness and My severity (see Rom. 11:22). My truth will be displayed in kindness but also in severity in this next era."

The Lord says, in this era, I am laying My righteous plumb line from heaven into the earth. The plumb line is My truth, for many have walked away from the truth and have perverted the truth. They have twisted My word to make it say what they want it to say. Many have said, "I will believe this scripture, but not that one." Others have said, "The Bible is simply written by mere man and carries no weight." Still others say, "The Bible is not relevant for today—it was for another era." But I say to you that My word is eternal in the heavens. The heavens and the earth shall pass away, but My word will never pass away (see Matt. 24:35). I have exalted My Word above all My name (see Ps. 138:2).

I have laid My plumb line into the earth and I am calling for an alignment of all things to this plumb line. My Truth will stand and all things must align. My kindness will draw you to turn away from a direction that is contrary to Me and My Word. I am filled with kindness, love, and compassion, but I am also a God of severity for I will not be mocked, and I will not allow My authority to be rebelled against. I am the Lord God Almighty and I will stand unwavering—My truth shall stand.

Ignorant men and women will say, "Oh, what does it matter? God will not care if I go the way of the world and love the longings of my flesh." These ones will be caught in the snares of their own passions, for what a man sows he will reap, and if he sows to the flesh, he will reap destruction. These ones are foolish and will suffer the consequence of their actions, for I am calling everything to align with Me— the plumb line of My truth.

Many of My people will have a fresh love for My Presence and for My Word. They will draw near to Me and I will draw near to them. They will read My Word with the eyes of the Spirit, and they will see glorious truth and wisdom within it that they did not see previously. They will have a fresh love for the Word as My Spirit reveals My will, and they will be doers of My Word. These ones will not compromise My truth, and I will honor them not only with blessing in this life but also with great reward in the eternal realm.

They will exalt My name and My Word without apology or shame and speak it boldly in the midst of contentious conversations. When they do, My plumb line will stand and those who align will be blessed. The proud and the arrogant will resist and rebel against My Word, but My humble servants will live by it no matter what the cost.

Those who choose to live by My Word and to align to My plumb line will know conflict because of the Word, but they will love Me and My Word more than the false peace that comes with the avoidance of conflict. I came to bring a sword that will divide.

Do not think that I came to bring peace on the earth; I did not come to bring peace, but a sword. For I came to set a man against his father, and a daughter against her mother, and a daughter-in-law against her mother-in-law; and a man's enemies will be the members of his household.

He who loves father or mother more than Me is not worthy of Me; and he who loves son or daughter more than Me is not worthy of Me. And he who does not take his cross and follow after Me is not worthy of Me. He who has found his life will lose it, and he who has lost his life for My sake will find it (Matthew 10:34-39).

This era will be treacherous, for there will be tension and war within the church because of My truth. Those who choose to raise the bar of sexual morality because of the instruction in My Word will pay a price, for those who will excuse and cover sin even in My own House will war against those who stand for the truth. Do not fear man or what he can do to you, for I will confirm and establish you.

After you have suffered for a little while, the God of all grace, who called you to His eternal glory in Christ, will Himself perfect, confirm, strengthen and establish you (1 Peter 5:10).

My Sword of Truth is My plumb line. Live by My Word. Allow My Word to instruct you. Love My Word. Do My Word, and you will prosper.

INSIGHTS

A discussion was taking place amongst a few of the younger generation and a couple of the older generation one evening in a church Bible study. The subject of sexuality came to the table and discussion was brought forward in regards to what the Bible said regarding homosexuality and the subject of fornication. A leader in the older generation shared from the scripture what God's Word taught on the matter and stated that this was the plumb line to which our beliefs are to align. He asked the group to express their thoughts on the verses. One of the younger generation, who grew up in the church and was a committed believer, spoke up confidently, saying, "But I don't believe those scriptures." Shock entered the room momentarily and she was asked to repeat it as the leader thought he was hearing wrong. She confirmed that she did not believe it. She explained that because she had gay friends whom she loved, she believed that God would love and accept them and their lifestyle without condition. Another in the group mentioned that many of the younger generation have open sexual relationships and that God created the body to enjoy sexual encounters so he felt it was acceptable. The leader was stunned as he was not expecting this, but then another of the younger generation spoke up in agreement with what the others had shared.

The leader asked if they did not believe the Bible, and they responded that they did believe the Bible but not those verses. Another questioned, "Wasn't the Bible written by men in their day? And now it's outdated and irrelevant, isn't it?"

I have spoken to other leaders who have had similar conversations with those in their congregation and ministry groups. It is alarming for sure. Many are questioning the Bible or even deciding to walk away from embracing it as the inspired Word of God. Others believe it has good portions in it and they pick and choose what fits their fancy. This is a dangerous hour. We must align to God's plumb line.

One of the most insightful Bible stories is that of Elijah confronting the prophets of Baal. I believe we are living in a similar day. Ahab was king and Jezebel was queen in Elijah's day. They had turned God's people away from the truth unto idols. Baal and the Asherah were sexual idols. The nation turned to these entities and hundreds of God's people became prophets (spokesmen) for Baal and for Asherah. It was a grievous day and Ahab and Jezebel were proud, arrogant, and defiant in the midst of it as they purposed to go their own way. They turned the nation away from God by disobeying the Word and making up their own rules.

Elijah came on the scene to challenge the deception. There were other prophets in the day who had not bowed their knee to Baal. I believe there are many believers today who have not bowed their knee either. Unfortunately, most of the other prophets in Elijah's day were hiding out in caves and not proclaiming the word. When we abdicate our authority to proclaim truth, we leave a gap for the enemy to fill. We cannot be afraid to speak the Word in this hour. I'm sure the prophets were afraid of the ramifications of speaking the truth, but we cannot shrink back—we must rise up and represent Jesus well, for He is the truth!

The Word is God's plumb line and we need to proclaim it and live it. Elijah did confront the prophets of Baal and Asherah and the power of God manifested. As a result of that confrontation, the false prophets—those who denied God's truth—lost their lives. May we see a company of believers who are radical and uncompromised like Elijah in this day. We are living in a serious hour. We must believe the Word, love the Word, and live the Word without shame or hesitation. God is aligning everything to His Truth. Man's agenda will not stand. In this next era, you will often hear the words, "Align,

align, align." It is important that we do, no matter what others say. The plumb line is in the earth—let's truly align.

Thoughts to Ponder

Do you believe that the Scriptures are the inspired Word of God? If not, why not?

Do you see a division line in society today between those who believe Bible values and those who do not?

What areas of division do you see?

Are you committed to God's plumb line of truth? If not, why not?

What ways can you be a voice to uphold God's Word in your realm of influence?

PRAYER FOR GOD'S PLUMB LINE

Heavenly Father,

I want to honor Your plumb line—Your truth. I ask You to keep me close to Your heart and close to Your truth. May Your kindness always lead me to repentance from anything that is not aligned with truth. May Your Spirit of truth fill me afresh every day of my life, revealing glorious revelation of Your Word to my hungry heart. Cause me to be bold and unwavering in my commitment to You and to Your Word.

In Jesus' name I pray,

Amen.

Chapter
Seven

AN ERA OF BIRTHING PRAYER

*Writhe and labor to give birth, daughter
of Zion, like a woman in childbirth.*
—MICAH 4:10

Prophecy

*Who has heard such a thing? Who has seen such
things? Can a land be born in one day? Can a nation
be brought forth all at once? As soon as Zion travailed,
she also brought forth her sons (Isaiah 66:8).*

In this hour, says the Lord, I will call My people into birthing prayer. There will be many who will be faithful to fast and pray, not for their own personal breakthroughs but for Mine. Through much intercession, groaning, and travail, I will give birth to My purposes in the nations in this hour. My

Kingdom will manifest in greater ways than the church has ever known, but it will not be birthed without much prayer.

I am looking for partnership. Together with the partnership of My people in prayer and intercession, My Kingdom will come and My will shall be done on earth as it is in heaven. In partnership with Me, you will see mountains move, you will see everything shaken that can be shaken, you will see My purposes manifest. It is not by might, it is not by power, but it is by My Spirit, says the Lord, and My Spirit will move as a result of the prayers of My people.

I will reveal the hidden things to My faithful intercessors. Even as I took My servant Ezekiel into the hidden places of the temple to see the abominations that were taking place in secret, so I will reveal these things to My faithful and they will sigh and groan over these abominations (see Ezek. 8–9). I will mark them, and I will empower them to bring down the strongholds and deceptions of the enemy so that My people will go free.

There are many of My people who suffer with weakness, temptation, and confusion and have been lured away from My truth, but My Spirit will help all who cry out in prayer with groanings in the spirit, for He will make intercession for the saints according to the will of God through the inner groanings of My people. Through deep intercession I will work all things together for good (see Rom. 8:26-28). Groan for your loved ones who are not walking with Me. Groan for those you see walking in rebellion, for My arm is not short that it cannot save. There is nothing too difficult for Me.

I am going to move in great power in the coming era and many shall be in awe of My majesty, but it will not come without the intercessors in their place. Have I not called all My people to intercession? Have I not said that, "If my people, which are called by my name, shall humble themselves, and pray, and seek my face, and turn from their wicked ways; then will I hear from heaven, and will forgive their sin, and will heal their land" (2 Chron. 7:14 KJV)?

I am calling My intercessors, My priesthood, into a place of groaning and travail. Many will be awakened in the night to pray and intercede, for I am putting My watchmen on the wall for such a time as this. Many will be called to fast from food, time, sleep, and pleasures in order to feast with Me in prayer partnership. I will gather many friends in this era—those who will partner with Me in prayer, those to whom I will reveal My secrets.

My intercessors shall rise up in great faith and they will be fearless. They will war, they will contend, they will break through. They will win battle after battle and secure My victories. They are relentless mighty men, women, and even children who love Me and who are called according to My purpose.

There shall be an increase of prayer houses in the nations. My people will gather and pray continuously to give birth to My purposes in houses of prayer around the world. It is a sober time and a desperate time, for there are many things that are being weighed in the balance in this hour. My intercessors will meet with Me at My mercy seat. They will call for mercy to triumph over judgment. They will call for the alignment of My people and will invite My conviction to fill the earth. Their prayers will be as incense and I will respond. Intercessors will give birth to a great move of My Spirit.

I will visit intercessors with great revelation and glory while they are seeking Me. Many will have rich and powerful encounters in My Presence that will astound them, for I will reward those who diligently seek Me. My intercessors will know what it is to come boldly before the throne of grace to obtain mercy and to find grace to help in time of need (see Heb. 4:16).

My royal priesthood, My intercessors, through travailing and persevering faith, will give birth to My promises and purposes. Through their persistence, lives will turn around, nations will turn around. It is a treacherous hour when men's hearts are being captured by lies and deception, but I have raised up those who will stand in the gap, raise the standard, and deliver My people. Destinies of nations will be birthed in this era, says the Lord.

INSIGHTS

Every child of God has been graciously granted the honor and privilege of bringing their requests before the Lord. He has promised to answer every prayer when we pray in faith according to His will. Let's rejoice over the following promises:

> *This is the confidence which we have before Him, that, if we ask anything according to His will, He hears us. And if we know that He hears us in whatever we ask, we know that*

we have the requests which we have asked from Him (1 John 5:14-15).

Therefore I say to you, all things for which you pray and ask, believe that you have received them, and they will be granted you (Mark 11:24).

For everyone who asks receives, and he who seeks finds, and to him who knocks it will be opened (Matthew 7:8).

Therefore let us draw near with confidence to the throne of grace, so that we may receive mercy and find grace to help in time of need (Hebrews 4:16).

And My people who are called by My name humble themselves and pray and seek My face and turn from their wicked ways, then I will hear from heaven, will forgive their sin and will heal their land (2 Chronicles 7:14).

We will sing for joy over your victory, and in the name of our God we will set up our banners. May the Lord fulfill all your petitions (Psalm 20:5).

Now, will not God bring about justice for His elect who cry to Him day and night, and will He delay long over them? I tell you that He will bring about justice for them quickly. However, when the Son of Man comes, will He find faith on the earth?" (Luke 18:7-8)

In this new era, the Lord desires His people to rise up in true priestly anointing that will bring birth to God's purposes, plans, and destinies in the lives of individuals and nations. The priesthood in the Old Testament stood in the gap before the people and the Lord, making sacrifices for their sins and bringing petitions before Him on their behalf. This is called "intercession," which is to represent someone else before God. In the New Testament we are called God's royal priesthood and are His kings and priests.

> *But you are a chosen race, a royal priesthood, a holy nation, a people for God's own possession, so that you may proclaim the excellencies of Him who has called you out of darkness into His marvelous light* (1 Peter 2:9).

> *And has made us kings and priests to His God and Father, to Him be glory and dominion forever and ever. Amen* (Revelation 1:6 NKJV).

In the previous decades, we have seen many intercession movements arise with large assemblies and stadium gatherings for prayer—prayer in the underground church of China, the prayer movement in Korea, and many others. One of the most recent and significant global prayer movements is the International House of Prayer (IHOP), birthed in Kansas City through Mike Bickle in 1999, where hour by hour, day after day, sometimes in an empty room, men and women, young and old, all races began to gather to a vision as simple in its essence as it was extraordinary in its scope—unceasing prayer with worship. "We will give everything!" they said, "even every hour of life itself—day and night!—to declare the supreme worth of Jesus to a jaded and unbelieving generation." By their twentieth year anniversary the organization had recorded over twenty million man hours of prayer and had hosted twenty thousand prayer missionaries on staff.[1]

Great things will be birthed by God through these committed intercessors, but God is calling all His people to the wall. Intercession goes before the hand of God moves. Intercession makes the way.

Joshua was mandated by God to lead the children of Israel across the Jordan into their promised land. The priests (intercessors) were carrying the ark of the covenant (representing God's presence and covenant promises). The priests stepped into the Jordan and the water parted so that all the people could cross over. The priesthood opened the way and gave birth to a new era for God's people as they entered into their land of promise.

> *"Behold, the ark of the covenant of the Lord of all the earth is crossing over before you into the Jordan. Now therefore, take for yourselves twelve men from the tribes of Israel, one man from every tribe. And it shall come to pass, as soon as the soles of the feet of the priests who bear the ark of the Lord, the Lord of all the earth, shall rest in the waters of the Jordan, that the waters of the Jordan shall be cut off, the waters that come down from upstream, and they shall stand as a heap."*
>
> *So it was, when the people set out from their camp to cross over the Jordan, with the priests bearing the ark of the covenant before the people, and as those who bore the ark came to the Jordan, and the feet of the priests who bore the ark dipped in the edge of the water (for the Jordan overflows all its banks during the whole time of harvest), that the waters which came down from upstream stood still, and rose in a heap very far away at Adam, the city that is beside Zaretan. So the waters that went down into the Sea of the Arabah, the Salt Sea, failed, and were cut off; and the people crossed over opposite Jericho. Then the priests who bore the ark of the covenant of the Lord stood firm on dry ground in the midst of the Jordan; and all Israel crossed over on dry ground, until all the people had crossed completely over the Jordan* (Joshua 3:11-17 NKJV).

Intercessors, it is time to arise in this new era. Partner with God to birth His glorious purposes, for it is truly time to give birth.

Thoughts to Ponder

As you review the promises of God regarding His desire to answer prayer, does it inspire you?

What is your prayer life like at this time?

Would you like more grace in order to increase your prayer life?

What steps could you take to improve your skills in prayer (i.e. training, activation)?

What areas of God's purpose and destiny would you like to see birthed in your life, in others, and/or in nations?

PRAYER FOR INCREASED ANOINTING IN PRAYER

Heavenly Father,

I desire to be an effective intercessor for You. I commit myself to You afresh and invite You to fill me with fresh empowerment to pray effectively in pure faith as I accurately hear Your Spirit's voice leading and guiding Me. Purify my heart and motives and empower to me to give birth to Your desires in the earth.

In Jesus' name I pray,

Amen.

NOTE

1. See https://www.ihopkc.org/.

Chapter
Eight

AN ERA OF GREAT FAITH

And without faith it is impossible to please Him, for
he who comes to God must believe that He is and
that He is a rewarder of those who seek Him.
—HEBREWS 11:6

Prophecy

In the scriptures, you will read accounts of great men and women of faith, but in this next era there will be a great company of powerful believers who will emerge in every nation and in every generation—these ones will be named and celebrated in heaven even as others that you see recorded as heroes of faith in My Word.

My servant Abraham moved My heart greatly because he believed, even though there was no natural evidence of what I promised him. I was invisible to him and My promises were invisible, yet he believed in My reality and in the tangibility of what I promised when I met with him. He took note of My presence and My voice. He believed My invisible appearance and obeyed what I called him to do. He was My son of great faith. Because he believed, I counted it to him for righteousness and called him the father of faith to those who believed after him. Without faith, it is impossible to please Me. Abraham pleased Me.

In this era, you will see the emergence of many who will acknowledge Me and believe Me with unshakable faith and determination—they will refuse to lean on their own understanding. They will refuse to listen to the opinions of others who attempt to water down and defy My Word and promises. They will refuse to waver in doubt and unbelief. They will stand on My Word, and when they have done all to stand, they will stand.

They will work miracles, signs, and wonders, for I will honor their faith and obedience as My Spirit leads them. As Elijah called down fire from heaven to display My mighty power and confront the enemy, so also will some in this new era, for they will not minimize My power or My ability. They will be filled with a holy jealousy for My name and glory. Daniel and his friends kept the faith, and in the midst of great opposition and deadly assault they believed. Even though they could have possibly lost their lives, they were determined to keep their faith strong in Me by refusing to bow to any idol no matter what the cost. As a result of keeping the faith, they saw great and mighty things. Did I not show up in the fiery furnace with them? Did I not shut the mouths of lions? I found faith in their hearts and I moved in power on their behalf. Many in this hour, like Daniel and his friends, will not bow, compromise, or be swayed.

In this era, I will call My people to possess great and precious promises, but some will stand in disbelief. Even as it was in the days when twelve of My sons went to spy out the land of promise, only Joshua and Caleb came back with a good report. They knew My promise and believed My promise. Caleb said in the face of the fear and opposition of the others: *"We should by all means go up and take possession of it, for we will surely overcome it."* But the men who had gone up with him said, *"We are not able to go up against the people, for they are too strong for us"* (Num. 13:30-31). Do not look at the obstacles before you and say, "This is too great for me." Do not look at the greatness of the promise I give you and think in your heart, "This will never be, for it is too great for me." Believe. Trust. Stand.

Great faith will produce great miracles and significant shifts in the spirit in this era. Great faith will produce transformation. Great faith will give birth to awakenings. A new wave of faith preachers will arise, and many of them will be of the younger generation. Some difficult times will come in this new era that will send shock waves through the nations, but I am calling those of great faith to turn people's hearts away from fear in those hours. My preachers of great faith will infuse the fearful with faith and call them to trust Me in the midst of the challenges they face. The enemy will cause the fearful to scatter, but I will call them to believe and will beckon them run to Me as their refuge and stronghold.

Some of those who will be honored for their great faith in this era will be children of tender age. I will appear to them in dreams, visions, and supernatural encounters, and they will believe and obey. They will speak what I reveal to them, and many will stand in awe and wonder. Some of the insights they receive will even make their way to government leaders and will grant the wisdom needed to resolve critical conflicts. Do not despise these little ones, for they will be known in heaven for their great faith. Do not squelch their faith, for that would be a serious transgression, but fuel it and empower it. Nurture these little ones and guard them as they mature in Me.

A new era is before you, and in this era I am looking for those of great faith—heroes of faith. Believe. Only believe and become one of great faith.

INSIGHTS

In the Word we see Jesus address issues of "no faith," "little faith," and "great faith." Obviously, most believers would want to please the Lord by having great faith. Let's take a look at each of them and discover what makes the difference between them.

No Faith

> On that day, when evening came, He said to them, "Let us go over to the other side." Leaving the crowd, they took

*Him along with them in the boat, just as He was; and other boats were with Him. And there arose a fierce gale of wind, and the waves were breaking over the boat so much that the boat was already filling up. Jesus Himself was in the stern, asleep on the cushion; and they woke Him and said to Him, "Teacher, do You not care that we are perishing?" And He got up and rebuked the wind and said to the sea, "Hush, be still." And the wind died down and it became perfectly calm. And He said to them, "Why are you afraid? Do you still have **no faith?**"* (Mark 4:35-40)

In this passage, the disciples who had already begun to walk with Jesus were invited by Him to go to the other side of the sea. He, along with the twelve, was in the boat sleeping when a powerful, fierce storm arose that had potentially damaging impact due to the waves breaking over and filling the boat with water. His disciples did not go to Jesus asking Him to silence the storm—they said, "Do you not care that we are perishing?" They had no expectation of victory—only of calamity. They had "no faith."

In the storms of life we face, we must remember that Jesus is "in the boat" with us and He has no intention of us perishing or being destroyed through any situation we might face. In fact, we are promised that *"God causes all things to work together for good to those who love God, to those who are called according to His purpose"* (Rom. 8:28).

If the Lord "called" His disciples to the other side, He would surely get them there. He will get you to where He has destined and invited you to go also. If there are battles or contrary storms along the way as we follow and obey His leading, He will overcome them.

The disciples were with Him, but they had no faith. Their expectation was that they were going to perish and that He did not care that they did. They had no faith to love through the storm and they had no faith in His love for them. No faith.

Little Faith

*For this reason I say to you, do not be worried about your life, as to what you will eat or what you will drink; nor for your body, as to what you will put on. Is not life more than food, and the body more than clothing? Look at the birds of the air, that they do not sow, nor reap nor gather into barns, and yet your heavenly Father feeds them. Are you not worth much more than they? And who of you by being worried can add a single hour to his life? And why are you worried about clothing? Observe how the lilies of the field grow; they do not toil nor do they spin, yet I say to you that not even Solomon in all his glory clothed himself like one of these. But if God so clothes the grass of the field, which is alive today and tomorrow is thrown into the furnace, will He not much more clothe you? You of **little faith**!* (Matthew 6:25-30)

In this situation, His disciples had uncertainty regarding provision. They had abandoned all, including their fishing businesses and tax collecting and medical careers to serve Him, and they had become worried about provision. They were used to working hard for their living, and I'm sure they were wondering how they were going to live as they became "fishers of men." In this case, Jesus evaluated their faith level as "little." They obviously had a measure of faith that they were walking in, but only a little, and that "little" was being addressed. Jesus wanted to assure them that all they needed would be provided for and that they were to look to God as their provider. They needed more faith.

Great Faith

> *And when Jesus entered Capernaum, a centurion came to Him, imploring Him, and saying, "Lord, my servant is lying paralyzed at home, fearfully tormented." Jesus said to him, "I will come and heal him." But the centurion said, "Lord, I am not worthy for You to come under my roof, but just say the word, and my servant will be healed. For I also am a man under authority, with soldiers under me; and I say to this one, 'Go!' and he goes, and to another, 'Come!' and he comes, and to my slave, 'Do this!' and he does it." Now when Jesus heard this, He marveled and said to those who were following, "Truly I say to you, I have not found such **great faith** with anyone in Israel"* (Matthew 8:5-10).

In this story we see the example of great faith. First of all, the centurion was a Roman and not a Jew. His servant was paralyzed and tormented, and the centurion knew exactly where to go for help. He had faith to approach Jesus, believing that he could have right standing with Him. He boldly approached Jesus who was obviously impressed already that a Roman would come to Him on behalf of his servant for healing.

When Jesus offered to go with him to heal the servant, the centurion replied that he did not need Jesus to come in person because he was convinced that all Jesus needed to do was to send the word. He understood and believed Christ's authority as the Son of God.

Jesus marveled at his faith. This faith involved the centurion believing in who Jesus was but also that His command was so powerful, He could just send the word and it would be done. Jesus called this "great faith." That is the kind of faith He wants us all to have. This kind of faith makes Jesus "marvel." *Great faith.*

In this new era, Jesus is calling for those who will *only* believe what He says. A phrase that I heard a powerful evangelist declare years ago was, "God said it, I believe it, that settles it." Let's make that a commitment for life.

Thoughts to Ponder

Do you have no faith, little faith, or great faith operating in your life?

Would you like to have an increase of operative faith in your life?

What areas in particular do you need breakthrough?

What can you do to build your faith in those areas?

"God said it. I believe it. That settles it" is a powerful statement of faith. Would you like to make this statement a solid and activated foundation in your life?

PRAYER FOR INCREASED FAITH

Heavenly Father,

I desire to be a faithful child who brings You great pleasure, and I know that when You see Your children walking by faith, it pleases You. Help me to grow in faith and to increase in my ability to believe.

In Jesus' name I pray,

Amen.

Chapter *Nine*

AN ERA OF DECREES

You will also decree a thing, and it will be established
for you; and light will shine on your ways.
—JOB 22:28

Prophecy

Who shall question My Word and its authority and power? Some will question, "Why should I believe the Bible? Why should I trust it, for is it not mere man who wrote it? Anyone can write a Bible, can't they? Why should I believe something that is not relevant to the times we live in or adherent to the new thinking of the day?"

My Word is truth and those who question it are foolish. My Word will direct and lead all who obey it into paths of righteousness and freedom, but those who deny will be ensnared. My Word is light and My Word is life.

My eyes are roaming to and fro to find those whose hearts are completely Mine and who will stand on My Word and proclaim My Word, for it is truth.

In this new era, I will find those who believe My Word and will trust its power to create, to settle battles, and to accomplish My will and purpose. They shall decree My Word in authority and faith, for they shall understand the weight and the infallibility of My Word. Did I not say that My Word will go forth and not return empty but will accomplish what I send it to do? (See Isaiah 55:11.)

In the beginning, I created the heavens and the earth by decreeing My Word. When I said, "Light be!" light appeared (see Gen. 1:3). The worlds were created with My Word, and by My Word and I will raise up a people in this hour who, like Me, will create and bring into being things that are not yet seen to the visible eye.

You will see limbs created before your eyes because My servants will command them to appear in My name and by My Word. You will witness eyeballs form in empty sockets and in bodies organs will be created that had previously been removed. You will see money fill bank accounts and unpaid bills will supernaturally be paid in full because My people will decree in My name and by My Word and it will be established.

When My Word is decreed in unwavering faith, the molecules, atoms, and subatomic particles will stand to attention and move in the direction they are commanded. They will revere My Word and obey it. As a result, there will be shifts in matter and miracle results will be seen. Many will stand amazed and will ask, "How can this be?"

For the word of God is living and active and full of power [making it operative, energizing, and effective]. It is sharper than any two-edged sword, penetrating as far as the division of the soul and spirit [the completeness of a person], and of both joints and marrow [the deepest parts of our nature], exposing and judging the very thoughts and intentions of the heart (Hebrews 4:12 AMP).

As My Word is decreed in this new era, many will align to My ways due to the conviction My Word brings to their hearts. It will pierce their soul and reveal hidden agendas and motives. It will separate the holy from the vile and cause light to arise and expel the darkness, for the entrance of My Word brings light (see Ps. 119:130).

The decrees of My Word will cause everything that can be shaken to be shaken. Decrees of My Word will bring exposure to hidden agendas of the enemy and cause spiritual battles to be won. Light will arise. My purposes will manifest. My glory will appear.

Decree. Decree. Decree.

INSIGHTS

A decree is an official order issued by a legal, governmental authority. It is different from both a confession and a proclamation in that it is brought forth through governmental initiation. It carries much more authority than a confession or proclamation. When you confess, you are admitting or testifying. When you proclaim, you are announcing something officially or publicly; but when you decree, you are speaking on behalf of God and declaring His Word. You are carrying out His orders.

In the Old Testament, a Hebrew word that is commonly used for *decree* is *kathab*, which is defined as "a written edict of royal enactment, of divine authority." We see an example of this word being used in Esther 8:8:

> *Now you write to the Jews as you see fit, in the king's name, and seal it with the king's signet ring; for a **decree which is written** in the name of the king and sealed with the king's signet ring may not be revoked.*

This powerful statement regarding a decree made in the name of the king can be applied to Jesus our King—He is, for all eternity, the King of all kings (see Rev. 19:16). There is no authority greater than that of Christ, and when you speak His word it carries incomparable weight and power—it will not be revoked!

Jesus taught us in Matthew 24:35 that His Word for all eternity will carry authority—even after heaven and earth pass. *"Heaven and earth will pass away, but My words will by no means pass away"* (NKJV).

Jesus revealed to His disciples in Matthew 28:18 that all authority in heaven and on earth had been given to Him, and as a result they were to go forward into the nations to make disciples. All authority has been given to Christ and His words are final, governmental words that can be decreed with confidence.

Decrees made in the name of Jesus are always based on the truth found in God's written Word and are spoken with bold, official, governmental, Kingdom authority that has been granted believers through Christ! We have God's written Word! The Bible is a book that is full of God's written decrees, and we can decree them with authority. It is interesting that when Jesus was in the wilderness being tempted by the devil, He responded to every temptation with, *"It is written"* (Matt. 4:4,7,10). He was decreeing the Word and settling the issues of temptation brought before Him.

Another Hebrew word translated as *decree* in the Old Testament is *gazar,* meaning "a decree, to cut off, to destroy, to exterminate." We find this word used in Job 22:28:

> *You will also decree a thing, and it will be established for you; and light will shine on your ways.*

In this chapter we find Job's friend, Eliphaz, condemning Job who had been going through a severe warfare crisis for months. Eliphaz was misapplying the principle of God's truth in regard to Job's situation. He basically was telling Job, "If you would get yourself right with God, you would then be able to decree a thing and your problems would be cut off, destroyed, and exterminated. Light would then shine on your ways and you wouldn't be in this mess you're in." He used the word to accuse Job of not having his heart right before God, but Job's heart was right, and later we find God rebuking Eliphaz for this judgment and inaccurate representation of His heart toward Job (see Job 42:7). However, the statement about the decree was correct—when you decree a thing, it will be established. Light will shine on your ways!

We see through this story of Job that when you make a decree you are "cutting off, destroying, and exterminating." This is a powerful way to engage in warfare. Decree the Word of God and let it go to work for you to destroy your enemies and their strategies. You will then be established in victory, and light will shine on your ways.

In John 6:63, Jesus said, *"It is the Spirit who gives life; the flesh profits nothing; the words that I have spoken to you are spirit and are life."* When you decree the Word that Jesus speaks, you are releasing life and power into the situation you are decreeing into.

I began creating decrees before I understood what they were. My husband was going through a discouraging time and had entered into a depression. One morning, he did not want to get up out of bed. I was concerned and knew he was struggling. As I prayed, I felt led to write out scriptures in first person so that he could read them over himself.

I wrote an entire page of scriptures that promised him victory over his discouragement and depression. I wrote declarations such as, "The Son has made me free and therefore I am free indeed" (see John 8:36); "God always leads me in His triumph" (see 2 Cor. 2:14), and, "In all these things I overwhelmingly conquer through Christ who loves me" (see Rom. 8:37).

Even though I lovingly prepared the declarations, in his depressed state he was not at all motivated to declare them. He just wanted to sleep. So I offered to decree them with him but lovingly insisted that he participate. He sat up in bed and at first barely whispered them. I honestly could not detect even a spec of faith as he read them through that first time, but when he finished he rolled over in bed intending to go back to sleep. I again insisted that he continue to read the declarations until he believed them and received them. We then decreed them a second time and then a third. By the third time through, he was already brighter and ready to get out of bed. The Word is powerful. I informed him that we would declare these scriptures again at least five times that day. In each of the five sessions, we proclaimed the decrees three times. The depression and hopelessness left in that one day of decrees and did not return.

After that successful shift that came about through the decreeing of God's Word, I began to create decrees often and for many circumstances. I found them to be consistently effective.

Prophetic Decrees

When you decree the Word over your life, you are releasing God's destiny plan and purpose. Here is a great scripture:

> *Thus says the Lord, the Holy One of Israel, and his Maker: "Ask Me of things to come concerning My sons; and concerning the work of My hands, you command Me"* (Isaiah 45:11 NKJV).

The first time I read this verse, it jarred me. I thought, "What? Command God? I can't do that." As I inquired of the Lord, He taught me that He desires us to seek His will concerning what He wants to do in our lives. When we discern it, He needs us to decree it. That is how we release the command of His will. I call these prophetic decrees. You first inquire of God concerning His will and then decree it. The decree is a command that is being released into the spirit realm to bring God's purposes to pass. When He hears the decree of His will released into the earth, He releases heaven to fulfill it.

In this era, we will see a new breed of prophets arise who will partner with God to bring His purposes into the earth. Some might think they are being presumptuous and overly confident, but they are simply operating out of Isaiah 45:11. They are releasing faith commands that activate the hand of God in the earth.

This era is an era of decrees. Our mouths shall open wide and decree the Word of the Lord.

> *But having the same spirit of faith, according to what is written, "I believed, therefore I spoke," we also believe, therefore we also speak* (2 Corinthians 4:13).

Thoughts to Ponder

Do you have an area of your life that could use an effective decree right now? Describe that area.

Inquire of the Lord in regard to that area according to Isaiah 45:11. What is He saying?

According to the outcome He revealed to you, create a decree based on His Word.

Decree out loud in faith numerous times until you have an inner witness that "it is finished."

PRAYER FOR CREATING DECREES

Heavenly Father,
Your Word is to be greatly honored, believed, and obeyed.
I desire to have more reverence for Your Word. Help me to
effectively inquire of You for areas of purpose in my life and
in Your Kingdom. Reveal Your will and guide me in the
creating and the declaring of Word decrees.
In Jesus' name I pray,
Amen.

Chapter *Ten*

AN ERA OF THE MANIFEST FEAR OF THE LORD

The Spirit of the Lord will rest on Him, the spirit of wisdom and understanding, the spirit of counsel and strength, the spirit of knowledge and the fear of the Lord .
—ISAIAH 11:2

Prophecy

Let all the earth fear the Lord: let all the inhabitants of the world stand in awe of Him (Psalm 33:8 KJV).

For the Lord Most High is awesome; He is a great King over all the earth (Psalm 47:2 NKJV).

Although I have poured out great grace and blessing upon blessing in these last days, many of My own people have neglected to reverence Me. They have not regarded or remembered My goodness and have been complacent and familiar with a God they barely know. Those in the world have arrogantly denied Me. They have spoken evil against Me and, carelessly in great pride, have without shame spoken vulgarities as they use My great name. They do not know Me, yet they foolishly misrepresent Me.

This is an era of alignment. Whatever is out of order must come into My divine order. I am going to send the Spirit of conviction, and when My conviction comes to the heart it must be embraced and not neglected or pushed away. It is time for the fear of the Lord to be restored to My people. It is time for the nations to tremble.

Many have neglected My commands and failed to obey the leading of My Spirit because they have regarded man more than they have regarded Me. They have held back because they feared the opinions of mere man. But I say, *"don't fear those who may want to take your life but nothing more. It's true that they may kill your body, but they have no power over your soul. The one you must fear is God, for He has both the power to take your life and the authority to cast your soul into hell. Yes, the only one you need to fear is God"* (Luke 12:4-5 TPT).

"The fear of man brings a snare, but he who trusts in the Lord will be exalted" (Prov. 29:25). For those who fear My name, I will arise with healing and restoration, but to those

who disregard Me it will be an hour when they will bear the consequence of their choices.

I will come to My people in this era as a refiner's fire and as launderer's soap, and I will purify My people and purge them of their unrighteous thoughts, words, and deeds.

"I will be a swift witness against sorcerers, against adulterers, against perjurers, against those who exploit wage earners and widows and orphans, and against those who turn away an alien—-because they do not fear Me," says the Lord of hosts (Malachi 3:5 NKJV).

"Your words have been harsh against Me," says the Lord, "Yet you say, 'What have we spoken against You?' You have said, 'It is useless to serve God; what profit is it that we have kept His ordinance, and that we have walked as mourners before the Lord of hosts? So now we call the proud blessed, for those who do wickedness are raised up; they even tempt God and go free.'"

Then those who feared the Lord spoke to one another, and the Lord listened and heard them; so a book of remembrance was written before Him for those who fear the Lord and who meditate on His name.

"They shall be Mine," says the Lord of hosts, "On the day that I make them My jewels. And I will spare them as a man spares his own son who serves him." Then you shall again discern between the righteous and the wicked, between one who serves God And one who does not serve Him (Malachi 3:13-18 NKJV).

My love is a purifying fire, and you will see My holy "love fire" burn up the dross of sin and impurity and separate My people unto Myself. My fire will both purify and reveal. The thoughts, intents, and motives of the heart will be revealed by the fire of My presence. Nothing will be hidden.

I will raise up many prophets in this era to proclaim My Word in power and conviction, for My Word is a fire, a hammer, and a sword. These prophets will speak without compromise that which comes from My heart and not what will simply tickle the hearts of those who hear. They will not say "Peace, peace" when there is no peace, but they will speak My truth because they will fear My name.

"For behold, the day is coming, burning like an oven, and all the proud, yes, all who do wickedly will be stubble. And the day which is coming shall burn them up," says the Lord of hosts, "that will leave them neither root nor branch. But to you who fear My name the Sun of Righteousness shall arise with healing in His wings; and you shall go out and grow fat like stall-fed calves. You shall trample the wicked, for they shall be ashes under the soles of your feet on the day that I do this," says the Lord of hosts (Malachi 4:1-3 NKJV).

In that day, many will proclaim:

How awesome are Your works! Through the greatness of Your power Your enemies shall submit themselves to You (Psalm 66:3 NKJV).

Days of awe are before you. Reverence Me in all your ways, for I am holy.

INSIGHTS

When you encounter the fear of the Lord, it changes you and the transformation goes deep into the inner recesses of the heart and mind. I think of Isaiah when he encountered the Lord:

> *In the year of King Uzziah's death I saw the Lord sitting on a throne, lofty and exalted, with the train of His robe filling the temple. Seraphim stood above Him, each having six wings: with two he covered his face, and with two he covered his feet, and with two he flew. And one called out to another and said, "Holy, Holy, Holy, is the Lord of hosts, the whole earth is full of His glory."*
>
> *And the foundations of the thresholds trembled at the voice of him who called out, while the temple was filling with smoke. Then I said, "Woe is me, for I am ruined! Because I am a man of unclean lips, and I live among a people of unclean lips; for my eyes have seen the King, the Lord of hosts."*
>
> *Then one of the seraphim flew to me with a burning coal in his hand, which he had taken from the altar with tongs. He touched my mouth with it and said, "Behold, this has touched your lips; and your iniquity is taken away and your sin is forgiven."*
>
> *Then I heard the voice of the Lord, saying, "Whom shall I send, and who will go for Us?" Then I said, "Here am I. Send me!"* (Isaiah 6:1-8)

At the time Isaiah had this encounter, he was already a seasoned and mature prophet, but one moment in the atmosphere of the fear of the Lord exposed things in his life that took him much deeper and prepared him for a greater assignment. He was undone when the fear of the Lord exposed the issues that needed to be addressed, but the Lord also had a plan to purify and remove the obstacles.

God wants us to embrace the spirit of the fear of the Lord and to invite His transforming presence to reveal our Christ-nature more than we have ever understood before.

In past historical revivals, such as the Welsh revival in 1904/1905, the spirit of conviction and the fear of the Lord was so present that lives were transformed overnight. The coal miners of the day were a rough bunch of characters who used profanities, were immoral in behavior, and were rough and crude in nature. The presence of the Lord's conviction hit them, and as a result they immediately repented and aligned with God's character and Word—they were true converts. History records that in some places in Wales, they had to close down the mines until they retrained the animals because the beasts of burdens only knew how to respond to cruelty and not to kindness. In the same revival, it is reported that bars and gambling houses closed due to lack of business. Prostitution ceased and court-houses closed because there were no criminal cases to try.[1]

The glorious presence of the fear of the Lord and His conviction were in the air.

Another account in church history is found in the First Great Awakening with Jonathan Edwards as he preached his famous sermon, "Sinners in the Hands of an Angry God." It is reported that Mr. Edwards delivered this sermon with a monotone voice as he read it slowly from his notes by candlelight in a somber manner. His pulpit presence was not at all impressive. He did not yell, scream, or shout.

In fact, he did not even gesture. The power was not in the delivery, but it was accompanied by great conviction of the Holy Spirit and the fear of the Lord.

As he spoke, men and women began openly weeping in the church. They shouted. Some screamed in horror. They interrupted him, yelling back at Edwards, "What must I do to be saved?" Some, it was said, white-knuckled the pillars and grabbed the pews fearing that, at any moment, they might tumble into the abyss.[2] Their lives were never the same again—they were transformed by His holy and awesome presence.

Similar accounts were reported in the Second Great Awakening with Charles Finney's ministry. A spirit of conviction and the fear of the Lord marked his revivals, and many converts not only turned to serve the Lord wholeheartedly but allegedly his revivals had a high retention rate of ongoing impact, sustained faith, and moral standards in the lives of those who were touched.

I have personally encountered the powerful, manifest presence of the fear of the Lord twice in my walk. It was glorious and never to be forgotten or minimized. There was such a tangible presence of the weight and glory of holiness that my body trembled to the inner core. I was literally afraid to move, think, or respond. I was very aware of the Lord's perfection and my imperfection and knew that I dare not transgress in even the slightest way in this holy presence.

Eventually the presence waned and I was able to rise off the floor, but I felt physically weak. I was aware of my need to draw close to the Lord, and even though His holy presence that produced the fear of the Lord was difficult to experience, when it waned I wanted Him to come back in that way. I long for that presence.

When the true spirit of the fear of the Lord comes on an individual, they are unable to sin. You dare not even think a sinful thought. Can you imagine the impact if a true and authentic visitation of the spirit of the fear of the Lord fell on the world we live in? Would sex traffickers be able to continue? Would drug cartels remain intact? Would corrupt leaders stand? What would the church look like if a visitation of the fear of the Lord filled it? Perhaps we would be like Isaiah—after conviction, purging; and after purging, a new level of assignment.

The Spirit of God is calling His people to birth through prayer a move of the fear of the Lord. Let's respond to the call. Let's hunger and thirst for a fresh infilling and empowerment that comes to us from the spirit of the fear of the Lord.

Thoughts to Ponder

Read and meditate on the following scriptures. Let them impact you.

> *The fear of the Lord is clean, enduring forever; the judgments of the Lord are true; they are righteous altogether* (Psalm 19:9).

> *The fear of the Lord is the beginning of wisdom; a good understanding have all those who do His commandments; His praise endures forever* (Psalm 111:10).

> *The fear of the Lord is the beginning of knowledge; fools despise wisdom and instruction* (Proverbs 1:7).

> *The fear of the Lord is to hate evil; pride and arrogance and the evil way and the perverted mouth, I hate* (Proverbs 8:13).

The fear of the Lord prolongs life, but the years of the wicked will be shortened (Proverbs 10:27).

In the fear of the Lord there is strong confidence, and his children will have refuge. The fear of the Lord is a fountain of life, that one may avoid the snares of death (Proverbs 14:26-27).

Better is a little with the fear of the Lord than great treasure and turmoil with it. …The fear of the Lord is the instruction for wisdom, and before honor comes humility (Proverbs 15:16,33).

By lovingkindness and truth iniquity is atoned for, and by the fear of the Lord one keeps away from evil (Proverbs 16:6).

The reward of humility and the fear of the Lord are riches, honor and life (Proverbs 22:4).

PRAYER FOR THE FEAR OF THE LORD

Heavenly Father,

I long to walk and live in the fear of the Lord all my days. Help me, Lord, to always reverence You and to walk in humility and honor before You. Fill me. Encounter me with the spirit of the fear of the Lord.

In Jesus' name I pray,

Amen.

NOTES

1. Carolyn Martel, "Donkeys confused without cussing," October 8, 2015. http://www.mymcr.net/opinion/donkeys-confused-without -cussing/article_9b9b9ea7-3cf8-5d58-9673-8888fc019003.html.

2. Tyler Scarlett, "Anniversary: 'Sinners In the Hands of An Angry God,'" July 7, 2018, https://www.forestbaptistchurch.org/ anniversary-sinners-in-the-hands-of-an-angry-god.

Chapter
Eleven

AN ERA OF THE CONSECRATED ONES

Then Joshua said to the people, "Consecrate yourselves, for tomorrow the Lord will do wonders among you."
—JOSHUA 3:5

Prophecy

My Kingdom is a righteous Kingdom. It is a holy Kingdom because I am holy. You will not find profanity or uncleanness in My Kingdom, and yet My people have chosen to bring mixture into My house.

Have I not said that the kingdoms of this world have become My kingdoms and I shall reign over them forever (see Rev. 11:15)? Have I not said in My Word to love not the world nor the things in the world, for if you love the world then the love of the Father is not in you (see 1 John 2:15)? Have I not said, "Come out of her, My people, lest you share in her sins, and lest you receive of her plagues"?

The devil is the god of this world and he has blinded the eyes of the unbelieving (see 2 Cor. 4:4), but the eyes of My people should not be blinded for I am their God and I have opened their eyes to behold Me, My Kingdom, and My righteousness.

My eyes are moving to and fro throughout the earth, to find those whose hearts are completely Mine that I might show Myself strong on their behalf (see 2 Chron. 16:9). My love has captured the hearts of many.

Therefore I urge you, brethren, by the mercies of God, to present your bodies a living and holy sacrifice, acceptable to God, which is your spiritual service of worship. And do not be conformed to this world, but be transformed by the renewing of your mind, so that you may prove what the will of God is, that which is good and acceptable and perfect (Romans 12:1-2).

This is an hour when hearts and the intents of the hearts will be revealed. It is an hour when I will separate good and evil, the holy and the profane, the flesh and the Spirit, the world and My Kingdom. It is a time of harvest when both the wheat and the tares will become evident.

It is time to consecrate yourself afresh unto Me and My purposes, for you are in the world as My salt and light but you are not of the world—you do not partake of its dark mindsets and deeds because you are of My light and you represent My light.

I am about to display a great wave of My authority and My great power and I am looking for a people whose hearts are completely Mine. I am looking for those who are completely consecrated unto Me, for they shall partner with Me to display great moves of My power and presence in this era. They shall be humble, not looking for their own glory and renown but Mine alone. They are My consecrated ones. They shall perform My exploits so that the world may know that I AM. All My children are invited to walk with Me in this way. Many are called, but only those who consecrate themselves will be chosen for what I am about to do in the earth.

There were many in David's day who could have been chosen, but David was My fully consecrated vessel and I chose him rather than his brothers. There was an army before Me in his day, but they did not believe Me. There was an appointed king in his day, but his heart was far from Me. David was My consecrated vessel, and although he was a young shepherd who tended the sheep, he was the one I chose to sit on the throne of My people. He was the one chosen to defeat Goliath. Although David was insignificant in the eyes of others, He had My attention. David was a man after My own heart, and I empowered him to perform exploits for My glory.

My son Joseph remained consecrated to Me in Egypt. Daniel and his friends remained separated unto Me in Babylon, and Elijah refused to bow to the idols of an evil king and queen. In this hour many people's hearts will harden and turn away from Me, but I am raising up My consecrated ones who will stand for Me with unwavering faith and conviction in this hour. They will refuse to bow to the god of this world or employ his tactics. They will flee temptation, for they are set apart ones.

In this era, you shall again discern between the righteous and the wicked, between one who serves God and one who does not serve Him (see Mal. 3:18). My fully consecrated ones are arising.

INSIGHTS

In the Old Testament, when an item was consecrated for use in the temple, it could no longer be used for mundane purpose, for it was holy unto the Lord. When we live a consecrated life, we understand internally that all we are and all we do is unto Him. We do not think, "This is Sunday, so I will go to church and be with God," and then live the rest of the week without regard for Him. When we are consecrated, we are joyfully aware of Him in all we do.

I love the story of Brother Lawrence. In 1640, at age 26, he became a lay brother in a monastery in France. Although he was very poor, uneducated, and socially awkward, many were attracted to his character and the atmosphere of divine peace that emanated from him due to his consecrated devotion to God.

His quest in life was to train his thoughts to think on God every moment of every day no matter what he was doing. For example, if he was washing floors, preparing meals, or fixing sandals in the monastery he would discipline himself to keep his mind set on the Lord in an attitude of worship and prayer. When he discovered a distraction from that focus, he would direct his attention back to God. He was committed to always being focused on an awareness of God's presence and engaged in worship and prayer. All he desired in life was to know and honor God, and he consecrated himself unto this purpose. Everything he did, no matter how mundane the task, was performed as unto the Lord in deep, committed love for Him.

You will empower what you focus on, and this was surely true regarding the undistracted focus of Brother Lawrence. The manifest glory of God followed him everywhere. People from all over came to the monastery to watch him wash dishes because the presence of God in the room was so tangible around him—God's "felt" glory presence literally filled the entire room where he was working and while he was working.

When asked what the formula was for approaching God, he said, "There needs neither art nor science for going to God, but only a heart resolutely determined to apply itself to nothing but Him, or for His sake, and to love Him only."

Brother Lawrence's letters and discussions with peers were later compiled into the book *The Practice of the Presence of God.* Even though he passed over 325 years ago, his teachings about prayer and pursing God's presence through a consecrated life are just as relevant today as they were in his day.

Here are some quotes that will help inspire you to practice authentic faith toward God and walk in the consecrated life.

> "We ought to propose to ourselves is to become, in this life, the most perfect worshippers of God we can possibly be, as we hope to be through all eternity."

"We should put life in our faith. We should give ourselves utterly to God in pure abandonment, in temporal and spiritual matters alike, and find contentment in the doing of His will, whether He takes us through sufferings or consolations."

"The more we know Him, the more we will desire to know Him. As love increases with knowledge, the more we know God, the more we will truly love Him. We will learn to love Him equally in times of distress or in times of great joy."

"One way to re-collect the mind easily in the time of prayer, and preserve it more in tranquility, is not to let it wander too far in other times: you should keep it strictly in the presence of God; and being accustomed to think of Him often, you will find it easy to keep your mind calm in the time of prayer, or at least to recall it from its wanderings."

"We ought not to be weary of doing little things for the love of God, who regards not the greatness of the work, but the love with which it is performed."

"There is not in the world a kind of life more sweet and delightful, than that of a continual conversation with God; those only can comprehend it who practice and experience it."

The Beauty of Knowing God

Knowing God is the sweetest, most beautiful and precious honor in life. Jesus pursued us with all He was and with all He had, and He continues to passionately pursue us to this day. He gave His life for us. He is in love! He set Himself apart for us, and we have the privilege of setting ourselves apart for Him with all we are and with all we have.

Consecration comes from a heart of love and is not birthed from religious pressure. Because He loves us, we love Him and consecrate ourselves for His holy purposes. This consecration is birthed through our personal desire and by His amazing grace that empowers us.

God's consecrated ones are being marked in this hour and they will manifest His glory to this generation. His presence along with signs and wonders will follow those who have given themselves completely to Him.

Thoughts to Ponder

What areas of consecration do you currently see established in your life?

What areas of your life need consecration?

What benefits do you believe to receive by further consecration of your life to God?

Do you have any struggles when you think about increased consecration of your life?

What are they?

PRAYER FOR CONSECRATION

Heavenly Father,

I fully dedicate and devote myself to You today and always.
Fill my life with great grace that enables me to walk out
a new level of consecration unto You without striving or
succumbing to religious effort. You are at work within me

both to will and to do of Your good pleasure. I give You my
fully consecrated life afresh.

Amen.

Chapter *Twelve*

AN ERA OF BREAKTHROUGH

So David went to Baal Perazim, and David defeated
them there; and he said, "The Lord has broken through
my enemies before me, like a breakthrough of water."
Therefore he called the name of that place Baal Perazim.
—2 SAMUEL 5:20 NKJV

Prophecy

I am the God of the breakthrough, and in this new era you will see My hand move on behalf of My people in astonishing ways. Many of My consecrated ones have been waiting for their victory and have stood faithfully before Me in unwavering faith trusting in My Word, yet they have not seen the manifestation of their breakthrough. But in this new era: *"Just as it is written, 'Things which eye has not seen and ear* has not heard, and which have not entered the heart of man, all that God has prepared for those who love Him'" (1 Cor. 2:9) shall be revealed by My Spirit and made fully manifest. Long-awaited breakthroughs will come forth in this era for the faithful.

Restoration of Losses

The enemy has come to steal, to kill, and to destroy and has devastated many lives, but this is the era of payback. This is the time when you will see My hand bring restoration to that which was lost, destroyed, or stolen in the previous season. You shall see the restoration of health, relationships, faith, finances, and possessions. You will not only see restoration of these things but you will see increase.

Look at My servant Job. Did not the enemy come to his house to steal, kill, and destroy? For a season, it appeared that the losses were established, but I am the God of the breakthrough and I broke through for him and restored all and even doubled his prosperity.

Reflect on My people who were held in bondage in Egypt, where they suffered the loss of wages due to cruel oppression. I brought breakthrough to them all *en masse* as I delivered them from the hands of their oppressors, but they did not leave empty-handed, for they plundered the Egyptians as they left. I restored unto them the wages they had lost over the years and led them to their own land—a land flowing with milk and honey and where they would not know scarcity. I restored their freedom to worship Me. I restored all, for I am the God of the breakthrough.

Enemies Defeated

As you draw near to Me and abide in Me, when the enemy comes against you one way, he will flee from you seven ways, for this is a season of breakthrough for you. The enemy will suffer loss at your hand and all will be recovered.

When My son David faced great devastation and loss at Ziklag, he inquired of Me in the midst of his discouragement. It appeared that all was lost and his own men blamed him. It appeared that the enemy had prevailed against both him and his people, but I am the God of the breakthrough and things are not always what they appear. When David inquired of Me in his despair, I answered, "Pursue, overtake, and recover all." He went forward in obedience and boldness and took back what was stolen. He defeated the enemy and recovered all. Like David, as you draw near to Me and inquire of Me, I will grant you the keys and instruction for your breakthroughs.

From Victims to Victors

In this era, many who had been victims of abuse, oppression, and failure will emerge as victors and champions, for My people are above and not beneath. They are winners and not losers. They are more than conquerors because I have already secured the victory for them and have given them power over all the power of the enemy. Victim mindsets shall be shattered and the lies of the enemy shall be exposed and demolished. I am the God of the breakthrough and I will grant the victor's crown to those who take My hand, walk with Me, and overcome.

Ambassadors of Hope Will Emerge

Many prophets will emerge in this hour as My ambassadors of hope. They will encourage My people to rise up in this new era and shake off the discouragements of the past. They shall reveal Me as the God of breakthrough to My people and grant them hope—a joyful expectation of good things to come.

There will be great shakings in this new era, but My Kingdom will stand and My faithful ones will be blessed in the midst of the shakings. I will hide them in My Presence, and they shall know My great love as I grant them breakthrough.

It is an hour for My holy ones to dream big and to know that I am a God who is able to do exceedingly abundantly above all you could ask or think according to the power that works within you. Your future is glorious as you draw close to Me, for I will break through on your behalf.

Breakthrough Discoveries

This is an era of breakthrough discovery. Through the revelation I release into the earth, there will be breakthrough discoveries that will be noted worldwide and will be broadcast for all to see. Mysterious discoveries in realms of science, medicine, and astronomy will materialize and be confirmed. Many shall be astonished and will stand in awe, for it is an era of discovery.

Look among the nations! Observe! Be astonished! Wonder! Because I am doing something in your days— you would not believe if you were told (Habakkuk 1:5).

Beware, as the enemy is lurking and desiring to use that which I release into the earth for his own evil purposes. Do not shrink back when you see this but keep your eyes on Me because I am the God of the breakthrough. At the end, all the enemy's works will be burned by fire, but all that is of Me will stand.

Remember that everything that can be shaken will be shaken, but you are of a Kingdom that cannot be shaken. The day will come when all will be revealed and judged, so do not be dismayed when you see the enemy's attempts to use for his evil purposes what I have created for good. His day of reckoning is coming, and he will suffer the loss of all things. But you will delight in My goodness, mercy, and abundance.

INSIGHTS

One of the greatest examples of breakthrough in the Bible is that of God's holy and faithful servant Job. The enemy had assaulted him in every area of his life and even turned his family and friends against him. He suffered great loss and it appeared that there was no breakthrough in sight, but in the end God granted not only an end to the attacks but a double restoration of all that was lost.

In the midst of the horrific assaults, Job postured himself before God, believing for breakthrough. The following principles found in Job's life will help us posture for breakthrough also when tragedy strikes.

1. Job worshiped in the midst of his assault (see Job 1:20).

Job did not take his eyes off of God during the season of testing and trial. His first response was to fall on his face and worship. Worship will keep your focus on the Lord and will connect you to His delivering presence. When you worship you become aware that He is all you need, and the battle is therefore diminished.

2. Job didn't blame God for the attack (see Job 1:22).

Often people believe that God authors assaults and tragedies, but He is a giver of life and goodness and not calamity. Jesus came to give us life in its abundance—it is the enemy who steals, kills, and destroys.

3. Job remained full of integrity in the midst of attack and challenges (see Job 2:3).

Trials and their many discouragements often cause individuals to compromise their faith and integrity. Many will quickly let their guard down, but Job did not. When you are assured of breakthrough, you will stand.

4. Job didn't come into agreement or alignment with the temptations and backslidden state of his wife (see Job 2:9-10).

When pursuing breakthrough, you must be careful not to partner with the negativity of those around you. There is one voice you must look for in a battle and that is God's.

5. Job watched over his mouth (see Job 2:10).

We are taught in the Word to "Let no corrupt communication proceed out of your mouth" (Eph. 4:29 KJV). During times of testing and assault, we must watch over our mouth. Words are powerful and we will be held accountable for every word we speak. The words we speak can aid in the release of our breakthrough or deter it.

6. Job's commitment to God trumped all (see Job 13:15).

In the midst of a trial, it is easy to get discouraged, anxious, and absorbed with temporal discomforts. Job's commitment to God was unwavering, and every other passion in life took a lesser place. When we are pursuing breakthrough, our eyes must be fixed on the God of breakthrough Himself and not on what we need breakthrough for.

7. Job believed God to redeem and resurrect him on the last day (see Job 19:25-27).

One of the keys to breakthrough is found in looking at the victory promised at the end of the battle. If your attention is fixed on the battle itself, you will become absorbed in the challenges and will weaken, but if you look to the final victory with eternal perspective you will be empowered.

8. Job didn't allow the negative and accusative words of his friends to affect him (see Job 16:2-5).

When you are in a season of assault, you are emotionally and mentally vulnerable and it is easy for the enemy to attack with accusation and condemnation. Oftentimes he will even use your friends and those close to you to deliver the arrows that pierce through into the heart. Job remained strong in the midst of the maltreatment by his friends.

9. Job was humble and honored the wisdom and counsel of God (see Job 42:2-5).

It is easy in the midst of assault and testings to lean to your own understanding, but we are to lean unto the Lord and seek His wisdom and counsel. Job had made some assumptions that he admitted were outside of truth, but he turned back to the counsel of God as soon as he realized this.

10. Job walked in forgiveness to those who were cruel to him and prayed for them (see Job 42:10).

The God of breakthrough gave Job his release from captivity when he prayed for his friends. Job freely forgave and breakthrough came. Unforgiveness, offense, and bitterness can hold you in captivity, but forgiveness releases you. When you pray for those who have hurt you, you are actually believing for their freedom and breakthrough from the deception they walked in toward you, and when you sow you will reap. Sow breakthrough and reap breakthrough.

Thoughts to Ponder

What areas of breakthrough do you currently need?

Do you acknowledge God as your personal God of breakthrough? If not, why not?

What lessons did you learn from Job's trial that can help you in yours?

If you were to "pursue, overtake, and recover all," what would that look like in your situation?

How can you get to know God in greater ways as your God of breakthrough?

PRAYER FOR BREAKTHROUGH

Heavenly Father,

I acknowledge You as My God of breakthrough. I invite you to fill me with power to partner with You in the midst of every adverse situation in my life. Grant me breakthroughs for the glory of Your name.

In Christ,

Amen.

Chapter *Thirteen*

AN ERA OF PERSECUTION FOR THE RIGHTEOUS

Blessed are those who are persecuted for righteousness'
sake, for theirs is the kingdom of heaven.
—MATTHEW 5:10 NKJV

Prophecy

In a day and hour when men's hearts turn to evil and when they take a stand against the Lord your God, I will raise up a people who are unwavering in their faith and commitment to Me. They will not fear for their lives or for what man will do to them. Some of the strongest, boldest, and most committed believers in church history will arise in this era, but their bold stand for the gospel will be accompanied by persecution and opposition to the truth. Even as those who persecuted Me, so shall they do to you.

When My Spirit is poured out, bold love comes on My people and they proclaim the gospel unashamedly, for it is the power of God unto salvation to everyone who believes. Many in this era will be willing to lay down their lives for Me. They will be willing to give up all for Me, for their hearts are entwined together in Mine and they will love as I love—they will be righteous as I am righteous.

As My gospel is preached with uncompromised conviction, it will cause division even in households, for My truth is a sword and will set a man against his father, a daughter against her mother, and a daughter-in-law against her mother-in-law. A man's enemies will be those of his own household. *"He who loves father or mother more than Me is not worthy of Me. And he who loves son or daughter more than Me is not worthy of Me. And he who does not take his cross and follow after Me is not worthy of Me. He who finds his life will lose it, and he who loses his life for My sake will find it"* (Matt. 10:37-39 NKJV).

Great rewards await those who are willing to stand for My truth, not only in this life but also in the eternal. For everyone who has paid a price to serve Me and *"has left houses or brothers or sisters or father or mother or wife or children or lands, for My name's sake, shall receive a hundredfold, and inherit eternal life"* (Matt. 19:29 NKJV).

Great Blessings for the Persecuted

Blessed are those who are persecuted for taking a stand for righteousness in this era, for theirs is the Kingdom of heaven.

Blessed are you when you are reviled and persecuted, and when evil is spoken against you falsely for My sake. In the midst of persecution, *"rejoice and be exceedingly glad, for great is your reward in heaven, for so they persecuted the prophets who were before you"* (Matt. 5:10-12 NKJV). The persecution will produce great fruit in your walk with Me, for after you have suffered for a little while, the God of all grace, who called you to His eternal glory in Christ, will Himself perfect, confirm, strengthen, and establish you (see 1 Pet. 5:10).

A greater division line will be seen in this era between the righteous and the wicked, for many will rise up with a strong deceptive voice in realms of business, media, government, and education. They will communicate values and formulate philosophies that are contrary to the Word, and they will attempt to pass laws in favor of their agenda.

It will appear for a season that the unrighteous are prevailing, but My verdict has already been set and the day will come when the saints of the Most High who have persevered will rejoice, for everything will turn in favor of My truth. My people will rise up with a strong, determined voice for righteousness and will see My truth prevail. They will be unwavering in their commitment and will be willing to face the loss of all things and to even be imprisoned for the truth they love.

In this era, martyrs will lay down their lives, for they will not bow or compromise. They will understand that no suffering in the present time can compare to the eternal glory that awaits them.

INSIGHTS

Persecution is never pleasant but is always life-transforming and rewarding. Some levels of persecution are definitely more severe than others, but if you are going to serve the Lord wholeheartedly, you will certainly experience some persecution. If you have never suffered even minimal persecution, perhaps you need to check your commitment thermometer to the gospel.

In the midst of persecution, you will be faced with two tests— faith tests and love tests. When Jesus came to the earth, He faced great resistance and persecution and His journey took Him to the cross. There were times when I'm sure it would have been easier to abandon His assignment, but He endured. In the garden of Gethsemane, He battled ferocious spiritual resistance to a point where He beseeched the Lord to remove the cup of suffering if possible, but He was not willing to disobey or fall short of the Father's will. From there He faced arrest and was brutally beaten, but He would not give up or give in. He was taken into an unfair trial where witnesses intentionally bore false testimony against Him, yet He did not open His mouth a word in His own defense. He was on a mission that would take perfect faith and perfect love, and He was not willing to withdraw either.

He was charged guilty of a crime He never committed and was stripped of His clothes, brutally scourged, and cruelly mocked. The masses were now convinced that He was guilty and was an imposter. The yelled out, "Crucify Him, crucify Him!" As He was nailed to the cross and hung to die, He looked out over the crowd and saw those whom He loved. There were those He healed, delivered, cleansed, and even raised from the dead standing before Him to judge Him as guilty and watch His execution. Where were His own? They had for the most part abandoned and forsaken Him, but in the mist of all His pain and suffering He never once lost faith in His mission or failed to walk in perfect love toward His enemies and those who opposed Him.

It would have been easy to lose sight of His mission and fail to believe in that hour. Everything looked contrary to the plan of Him becoming the Savior of the world and the King of kings and Lord of lords, but He went to His death believing that the Father would raise Him from the dead on the third day. He also went to His death in perfect love. Some will forgive those who are cruel to them, but few will lay their lives down for those who mistreat them. Jesus did both. He forgave, refused to judge, and paid the price for our full redemption. He became our sin and gave us His righteousness—all for free.

He was cruelly persecuted throughout His entire life, but He remained strong and unwavering in both faith and love. As a result, He now lives in His eternal reward! He is forever King over all!

Throughout your journey with the Lord you will face opposition and persecution, and like Jesus you will be invited to pass your love tests and your faith tests. It is beautiful and of course a great honor to suffer persecution for the truth, although it is never pleasant at the time.

One of my seasons of persecution was following a time when I had encountered the Lord in a glorious thirty-day visitation. During the visitation, He revealed and confirmed to me the free access that was available to all believers into the realms of His glory in the heavenly dimension. Day after day I enjoyed truth encounters and experienced divine engagements. It was truly glorious.

Immediately following this visitation, I began to share the very things the Holy Spirit had taught me with whoever was hungry to learn. Every time we would gather, He would bless us with magnificent manifestations of His glory and holy encounters. It was so wonderful. Door after door opened due to the intense hunger of God's people.

After about eleven months of teaching on the glory, I hit some major opposition from significant leaders in the Body who accused me of being deceived and deceiving the people. I was called rebellious, controlled by a Jezebel spirit, and a false prophet and teacher. My character was in question also, and I was told I was leaving a mess behind in every place I ministered.

I was overwhelmed and undone. I had never been rebellious or defiant (even before I gave my heart to the Lord) and I was not aware of any "mess" I had left behind. When the initial wave hit, I chose to go low and not defend myself. I laid down my ministry for a few months until I could complete a theological audit through a credible theologian who carefully reviewed all my teaching, a character audit (by following up on everywhere I had ministered and inviting my family and team to scrutinize me), and a prophetic audit (to assure I was in the right prophetic timetable and not running ahead of God).

After the four months, every audit was complete and there were literally no issues or concerns presented. In many cases there was great affirmation. This gave me personal confidence and relief, but it did not end the persecution. In fact, the persecution continued for over nine years. It intensified and spread into global spheres of influence through well-known ministers. At the time, if you looked on Google for my name, the first twenty pages or so were filled with negative headlines and remarks about my name, teachings, and ministry.

I knew that I was mandated to open up a portal for the supernatural, but the persecution was brutal. When you are called, the call is greater than you, and it is difficult to lay down even if you desire to in your natural mind. Many questioned my integrity, the accuracy of my message, and the authenticity of my love for God. In the midst of it, I knew I had to finish the assignment. The Lord reminded me to keep the faith and to walk in love without wavering and without hypocrisy. He made it clear that I was not to attempt to defend myself but rather to walk in humility, honor, and love toward those who were in opposition.

It was a painful but beautiful journey. I learned to fellowship with Christ's sufferings—His love sufferings. He taught me so much in that season and I am forever grateful. In the natural you would think that all would be lost through that level of persecution, but instead our ministry grew, our team grew, and God promoted us to greater honor than we had ever known. Eventually those who had stood against me in that season asked forgiveness, and for the most part we all walk well together and some of them are very close friends and honored and treasured comrades in the faith. It is so beautiful.

One day as I was thanking God for His wonderful faithfulness during that season, He said, "But you haven't seen anything yet—your greatest rewards are to come." I weep thinking of that. It is such an honor to serve Him and to suffer for Him (although my suffering is very minimal compared to many), but to think that He rewards it in such great ways is mind-boggling.

Persecution has taught me much—there are so many lessons to learn through what we suffer. Oh, that we might know Him!

Thoughts to Ponder

Reflect on your walk with the Lord. Have you suffered persecution for your faith?

What did the persecution(s) look like? Describe.

What faith tests did you pass?

What love tests did you pass?

What did you learn through persecution?

PRAYER FOR EMBRACING PERSECUTION

Heavenly Father,

I come before You and ask for grace to embrace persecution when it comes. Help me to be strong in the midst of it and unwavering in my faith and love.

In Jesus' name I pray,

Amen.

Chapter *Fourteen*

An Era of Divine Wisdom and Counsel

If any of you lacks wisdom, let him ask of God, who gives to all liberally and without reproach, and it will be given to him.

—James 1:5 NKJV

Prophecy

I have opened My throne for My people to approach Me and freely receive My wisdom and counsel. By faith, come boldly before My throne and obtain the counsel that you need, for it will not be withheld. Many have leaned on their own understanding without inquiring of Me in the midst of difficult situations, but My counsel is always available. Simply come.

Receive. Issues will be settled in your favor. Battles will be settled on your behalf as you come and receive My wisdom and counsel.

In this era, great wisdom will be needed to resolve conflicts and great wisdom will surely be given to those who seek after it for it will not be withheld. *"Wisdom is the principal thing; therefore get wisdom. And in all your getting, get understanding"* (Prov. 4:7 NKJV).

Discoveries and Solutions

I have many things to reveal to those who come to Me, for this era will be an era of discovery and it will be an era of solutions. I have things to reveal that have been hidden from man's understanding until this hour. These hidden things are to be discovered by those who seek My wisdom and counsel.

There are many leaders around the globe who meet together at their council tables to discuss problems and solutions, but they fail to understand that I am the One with the answers they are looking for. I am the One who grants wisdom and counsel. I am the One who grants understanding. And when My wisdom and counsel are absent, then folly appears. Many foolish decisions have been made by man to bring forth what appears like a solution, but they only cause further harm. They see relief for a moment and believe it is settled, but over time their solutions destroy because they are contrary to My wisdom and counsel. This wisdom is not that which comes down from above, but is earthly, natural, demonic (see James 3:15). The way of a fool is right in his own eyes, but a wise man is he who listens to My counsel (see Prov. 12:15).

It is time to seek Me, for I will grant divine solutions and divine intelligence to those who will humble themselves and pray. I will withhold no good thing to those who seek Me with a sincere and believing heart. Do you have a problem? I have the answer. Do you need insight? I have counsel for you. I wait for you to come, to embrace, and to receive My counsel.

Great Wealth Coming Forth

Long life is in wisdom's right hand and in her left hand are riches and honor (see Prov. 3:16). Yes, riches and honor are with wisdom, enduring wealth and righteousness, so pursue My wisdom with your whole heart (see Prov. 8:18).

I am releasing great wealth and increase to many who embrace My wisdom in this era, for I am the One who gives you the power to make wealth, that I may confirm My covenant which I swore to your fathers, as it is this day (see Deut. 8:18). In days of challenge when many would fear, those who seek My wisdom and counsel will be positioned to receive My bounty and abundance.

Family Issues

Many who face challenges in their marriages or with their children will go to a therapist, doctor, counselor or coach, but I have never seen them. They have never come to seek My counsel or to receive My answers. I am watching over them, waiting for them to come and receive. I knock on the door of their hearts, saying, "Come to Me," but they do not come. They cry out to Me in their anguish but they do not seek My counsel. Instead they say, "I must make an appointment with a doctor, counselor, coach, or therapist to receive some help and relief." But your help comes from Me. I am your very present help in time of trouble (see Ps. 46:1). Come to Me and wait on Me for My direction. I will give it.

Everyone who asks for wisdom will be granted wisdom in abundance, for I will not withhold it, but you must come in faith without wavering in unbelief or doubt.

> *For the one who doubts is like the surf of the sea, driven and tossed by the wind. For that man ought not to expect that he will receive anything from the Lord, being a double-minded man, unstable in all his ways* (James 1:6-8).

> *Counsel is mine and sound wisdom; I am understanding, power is mine* (Proverbs 8:14).

Come to Me and I will lavish you with My wisdom and counsel. Many will be astonished in this era as to the extraordinary wisdom and solutions that will be made known.

Do you need My wisdom and counsel right now? It is available to you. Come.

INSIGHTS

From the early days of knowing Christ, I hungered for wisdom. As a result, for a number of years, I read through the first eight chapters of Proverbs daily and feasted on the Word, longing for an impartation of

God's wisdom, counsel, and understanding. A number of years later, during a ministry engagement in Coeur d'Alene, Idaho, I was visited by an angel called Wisdom while engaged in my morning prayer and devotion time. Angels are ministering spirits sent by God to minister to His children (see Heb. 1:14). I believe that an angel of wisdom was assigned to me that day, but even greater than an angel of wisdom is Jesus Himself who has become wisdom to us (see 1 Cor. 1:30). All we need in life is Jesus, for He is our all in all; and our first love, our first expression of honor, and our deepest adoration is to Him, but He does direct precious angels to serve us at times. We are to be grateful for angelic assistance and presence, but they are never to be worshiped or even slightly compared with Jesus who is all things to us and worthy of all.

I have very much enjoyed walking with and in God's wisdom. When I would seek Jesus specifically for wisdom concerning a situation, as I waited, wisdom would suddenly come into my understanding. In like manner, as I was in leadership meetings regarding conflicts that needed to be resolved or obstacles that needed to be overcome, the solution would unexpectedly enter my mind.

Wisdom has been invaluable over the years and has offered solutions and insights into many challenging situations. When our ministry was initially led by the Lord to help those oppressed by sex slavery, I was directed to engage in a scouting trip to Thailand. One day while in Pattaya (a world-renowned city known for sex tourism) I was deeply burdened with what I saw. There were so many young girls working in the bars and brothels. After interviewing a number of them, I became aware of their painful stories—many of them had been brought to work in the brothels by their own parents in order to make income for the family. Bars and brothels lined the streets and all of them "employed" girls. The streets were full of sex tourists visiting from the nations, looking for "merchandise."

After the first day of walking the streets in Pattaya, I was emotionally overwhelmed. I wanted to leave Thailand and never return. The problem seemed so massive, and I could not see the solution. In my hotel room later that day, I cried out to God in my anguish and He heard me. I desperately wanted to leave, but He wanted me to become a solution. Suddenly wisdom poured into my heart and I was empowered through it. It was simple at first. He questioned me, "Is My light able to penetrate darkness?" The answer was an obvious, "yes," but then I was confronted on why I did not believe He was well able to help me to be part of the solution and to overcome.

The next evening, we joined with a local ministry to go into a bar/brothel. It was Valentine's Day, and the church's worship team offered "free entertainment" (love songs) for Valentine's Day. (They neglected to mention to the establishment that they were "Jesus Love Songs.") The brothel owner was delighted to have the free entertainment. While the worship team "entertained," we sat with the girls at the tables, buying Coca-Cola and listening to their stories. We shared the gospel with them, prayed, and gave them hope.

The Holy Spirit directed me through His wisdom to give some prophetic words to those in the bar/brothel. Because it was still early, most of the bar was filled with workers and not many customers. I asked the brothel owner if I could share some words about people's futures. She said, "Oh, you are fortune teller!" (Many of the Thai people love fortune tellers.) I explained that I was not a fortune teller but that I knew God and He was giving me encouraging words about people's futures (destinies). She replied, "Yes, you fortune teller." At that point, I thought that if I could get the microphone, she could call me a fortune teller—at least I would get the microphone.

I began to point out specific people whom the Holy Spirit highlighted and publicly, through an interpreter, gave them words. They were impacted and openly showed it through delight and tears in some cases. I then invited anyone who desired a word of blessing from God to come forward and I would give words to anyone who desired them. A substantial line came up to the front, and I prophesied destiny over each one. We then gave them opportunity to give their lives to the Lord. Some received and were followed up on by the local ministry.

When I returned to my room that night I was filled with fresh hope and vision. The wisdom of God visited me again and showed me an effective plan we could move forward with. In just a few months we returned to Thailand with our School of Extreme Love. We gathered believers from the nations to reach out in love to the girls in the brothels. We hosted banquets for them, networked with local ministries for follow-up, and established a full-time team member in Pattaya. We soon came to realize that there was so much more than only the girls in the brothels. There were boys and also young children, some were even infants, who were trafficked and enslaved. Many of the young children were from Cambodia, and there were no protections or advocates for these children at the time. Our worker met with the United Nations and with government leaders in both Thailand and Cambodia demanding some reform and protection for the Cambodian children. God filled her with "wisdom from above."

As a result of her labors and following the divine wisdom of the Lord, she was able to build a Christian team of traffic police, social workers, and attorneys and bring about policies to protect the children. I am very proud of her and she now is the global head against child trafficking and exploitation for a network of over 100 organizations. The wisdom of God led her, gave her understanding and counsel, and supernaturally opened doors for her.

The wisdom of God further directed us to set up a base in Cambodia to help eliminate the trafficking of children and to establish health in the nation. Systemic poverty is one factor involved making children vulnerable to be sold into slavery by their parents. God gave us wisdom on how to come against that by building businesses and offering employment. He gave us wisdom on how to transform the slum areas that were the most vulnerable. Wisdom taught us to put feeding and education programs in place, to build prayer houses and churches, all that brought light into the darkness.

Over and over we have seen the wisdom of God lead. Wisdom was with God when He created the earth. Wisdom is a master builder. Wisdom is a person—Jesus Christ. *"But of Him you are in Christ Jesus, who became for us wisdom from God—and righteousness and sanctification and redemption"* (1 Cor. 1:30 NKJV). As we worship and adore Him, understanding that He has become wisdom unto us, our lives will never lack the wisdom that is needed for any circumstance we face. In this era, we will see wisdom at work. We will see Jesus at work. Let's position ourselves to receive.

Thoughts to Ponder

Jesus has been made wisdom, righteousness, sanctification, and redemption for you. Worship Him. All wisdom is in Him.

Is there an area(s) you need wisdom in at this time? Describe.

Have you made decisions in the midst of conflict and crisis without seeking God's wisdom and counsel first? If so, why?

Are you willing to make seeking God's wisdom and counsel a priority?

What things will help you receive His wisdom?

PRAYER FOR DIVINE WISDOM AND COUNSEL

Heavenly Father,

You say in Your Word that if I need wisdom, I can ask of You and You will give it to me. Forgive me for any time in the past when I failed to seek You first before making decisions. I receive Your love and forgiveness. I ask that You fill me with wisdom today and always as I make wisdom a priority.

In Jesus' name I pray,

Amen.

Chapter *Fifteen*

AN ERA OF THE REVEALING OF THE BRIDE

Let us rejoice and be glad and give the glory to
Him, for the marriage of the Lamb has come
and His bride has made herself ready.
—REVELATION 19:7

Prophecy

"Who is this coming up from the wilderness, leaning on her beloved?" (Song of Sol. 8:5). It is My lovely Bride, for she is being awakened and revealed in this hour. Her heart is alive with love and she desires nothing less and nothing more than Me. She has ravished My heart.

In this era, you will behold those whose passion for Me will be ignited in deeper ways than they have ever known. Their love for Me will be as a flame that ever increases. Deep will call to deep within them. The more they encounter Me, the more they will desire Me. And the more they desire Me, the more they will encounter Me.

My Bride is altogether glorious, for her heart is fully Mine. She is pure, holy, and God-fearing. She is patient and kind. She is gentle and meek. She is submissive, obedient, and full of courage. She is industrious and resourceful. She is faithful and full of faith. She is beautiful beyond description, magnificent in glory, and clothed in My love. Oh, do you see her unfolding? I am revealing her in this hour.

There are many who say, "I believe in Jesus—He is my Savior," but I do not know them, for their hearts are far from Me in their daily walk. Other things absorb their attention. They have failed to relinquish the rule of their lives unto Me and give very little place to My ways and direction. They deliberately continue in sinful practices they know are forbidden in Scripture and do not even seem to be concerned about it. My church is full of those who gaze on pornography, commit fornication and adultery, are involved in homosexuality, have abortions, get drunk, and abuse drugs. They lie, cheat, steal, engage in pride, gossip, unforgiveness, and slander and are disobedient to My great commission. These ones have one foot in the world and one foot in My Kingdom. These ones love fleshly indulgences more than Me. They say, "I am redeemed by His blood and all My sins are forgiven" while they are yet in the midst of sinful practices. They speak arrogantly and they are ignorant of the truth.

They do not embrace the attributes of My Bride, but many of them shall come under conviction in these days and will turn their hearts back to Me. They will abandon their worldly passions and lusts and return to Me. They will prepare for My coming and will become gloriously arrayed in My presence and truth. A fire will burn with intensity within them—the fire of My love—and they shall turn.

I am knocking on the hearts of My people. I am calling for My beloved Bride to awaken and she shall. You shall see her emerge. In this era, those who are My Bride will prepare—they will make themselves ready.

INSIGHTS

The Bible is a beautiful love story revealing the Father's search for a Bride for His Son. We see the story unfold in the first book of the Bible when the Father spoke concerning Adam, *"It is not good for the man to be alone; I will make him a helper suitable for him"* (Gen. 2:18). Throughout the Scriptures we see this theme continue all the way to the final chapters in the Bible, describing this perfect Bride who made herself ready. The Bride longs for her Bridegroom. Her heart is toward Him all day long and she yearns for and calls for His return. The Bible closes with the cry of the Bride: *"The Spirit and the bride say, 'Come'"* (Rev. 22:17).[1]

Jesus is coming for a Bride that is expecting and longing for His return. He teaches us in His Word to be ready even though we do not know the day or the hour—the Father alone knows. When the Father tells His Son to collect His Bride, He will suddenly come. We see a picture of this in the following story.

> *Then the kingdom of heaven shall be likened to ten virgins who took their lamps and went out to meet the bridegroom. Now five of them were wise, and five were foolish. Those who were foolish took their lamps and took no oil with them, but the wise took oil in their vessels with their lamps. But while the bridegroom was delayed, they all slumbered and slept.*
>
> *And at midnight a cry was heard: "Behold, the bridegroom is coming; go out to meet him!" Then all those virgins arose and trimmed their lamps. And the foolish said to the wise, "Give us some of your oil, for our lamps are going out." But the wise answered, saying, "No, lest there should not be enough for us and you; but go rather to those who sell, and buy for yourselves." And while they went to buy, the bridegroom came, and those who were ready went in with him to the wedding; and the door was shut.*
>
> *Afterward the other virgins came also, saying, "Lord, Lord, open to us!" But he answered and said, "Assuredly, I say to you, I do not know you."*
>
> *Watch therefore, for you know neither the day nor the hour in which the Son of Man is coming* (Matthew 25:1-13 NKJV).

In this parable there were ten virgins with a number of things in common:

- They were all expecting the bridegroom.

- They all had lamps.
- They all heard the shout at midnight.
- They all went out to meet him.

However, there was one significant difference: five of them were ready and five of them were not.

The five that lacked fresh oil for their lamps ran to get it at the last minute, but it was too late. When they came to the wedding feast later, after they bought their oil, the door was already shut. They cried out, "Lord, Lord, open up for us." He replied, "I do not know you."

The Bride of Christ is a wise virgin. She awaits her Bridegroom with oil in her lamp. In Scripture, "oil" represents the anointing of the Holy Spirit who comes and fills us to overflowing with His Presence. The easiest way to be filled is simply to spend time with the Lord. We see a picture of this in Psalm 23. The Lord welcomes us to His banqueting table where we meet with Him in intimate communion. As we do, the Word says He pours out His oil upon us until we overflow like a cup that has been filled beyond its brim (see Ps. 23:5). To make sure you are full of fresh oil, spend time with God. Here are three simple ways you can do that every day:

1. Read your Bible! Scripture is more than print on a page, it is the Living Heart of God revealed. As you get into the Word, the Word gets into you—filling you with His Truth until you overflow with Him everywhere you go!

2. Worship! When we worship the Lord, we are turning our hearts to Him, drawing near to declare our love and appreciation of what He has done, and of who He is. In James 4:8 the Lord promises that as we

draw near to Him, He will draw near to us. When we praise and worship, it is like singing an enthusiastic "Yes!" to the invitation of Psalm 23 to come and sit with Him. We cannot help but be filled with His presence!

3. Pray! Any good relationship is built from good communication. Prayer is talking with God, sharing your heart with Him, and taking the time to let Him share His heart with you. Like with worship, to talk with God is to draw near to God. When we do, He draws near to us—filling us afresh with His presence. When we turn to the Lord in prayer, we become like John the Beloved, leaning against the breast of Jesus. So close. So intimate, we can hear the very beating of His heart, that glorious heart of His that beats for each and every one of us!

Who Is the Bride of Christ?

Some state that the Bride of Christ is made up of all believers. Others are convinced the Bride includes the Jews who have received the Messiah. Some believe that the Bride is made up of Christians living at the time of the rapture, and yet others are convinced the Bride is a consecrated remnant within the Body who are waiting for the return of the Lord. I am certain the Lord wants His Bride to include all believers, yet I personally do not sense that all will be included in His Bride. God alone knows the heart of each individual. He knows if your heart is completely His or not. The Scripture clearly teaches that the Bride of Christ "makes herself ready." She will have a heart only for Him and will have no other gods or idols.

This single-heart focus is the main quality of the Bride. My personal conviction is that the Bride is a remnant within the Body of believers who is completely consecrated unto the Bridegroom and who is obedient to His Word. Those in this remnant have made themselves ready by watching over their hearts with all diligence. They love, serve, and obey Him in complete abandonment; are not legalistic or religious in their motivation; and neither are they bound by self-righteousness. They live with this focus of complete abandonment because they love Him. They believe the truth about Him and know He is worthy and deserving of their all.

Jesus is marrying a Bride who has made herself ready, a Bride who has eyes only for Him. He is marrying a Bride who wants nothing else in life but to know Him, to be intimate with Him, to live with Him and to serve Him and with Him forever. He is marrying a Bride who does not love the world or the things of the world. She is fully separated unto Him and Him alone. She loves the things He loves and hates the things He hates. She longs for the return of her Bridegroom and is watching for His coming. This is the heart of the Bride of Christ. Jesus will rule and reign with His Bride for eternity.

The Lord is alerting His church in this hour. It is time to prepare for a glorious day—the wedding of Jesus the King and His glorious Bride. He is coming for His Bride. A wedding feast is being planned by our heavenly Father. At this celebration there will be guests in attendance and the Bride and Groom.

Then he said to me, "Write, 'Blessed are those who are invited to the marriage supper of the Lamb'" (Revelation 19:9).

It will be wonderful to be invited to this event, but oh, to be the Bride and not just an invited guest!

May you enjoy being filled with His precious love and grace as you prepare for this glorious day. When is the day? When is the hour of His coming for His Bride? Only the Father knows, but His Bride is making herself ready.

The Spirit and the bride say, "Come" (Revelation 22:17).

Thoughts to Ponder

The marriage of the Lamb is likely the most important event in eternity next to Christ's finished work on the cross.

Are you stirred with deep hunger and thirst for your Bridegroom's presence? If not, would you like to be?

What attributes of the Bride of Christ do you identify in yourself?

If Christ were to come today for His Bride, are you ready?

How would you like to prepare for Him?

PRAYER FOR BRIDAL PREPARATION

Heavenly Father,

I long to be ready when Christ comes for His Bride and I commit myself to becoming ready. Increase Your grace upon my heart and teach me how to walk as Christ's glorious Bride.

In Jesus' name I pray,

Amen.

NOTE

1. Patricia King, *The Bride Makes Herself Ready: Preparing for the Lord's Return* (XP Publishing), Kindle loc. 30-33.

Chapter *Sixteen*

AN ERA OF HARVEST

*And another angel came out of the temple, crying
out with a loud voice to Him who sat on the cloud,
"Put in your sickle and reap, for the hour to reap
has come, because the harvest of the earth is ripe."*
—REVELATION 14:15

Prophecy

For generations, My people have sown My Word into the earth. The gospel has been proclaimed in the nations as precious seed. Many labored in dark fields, sowing faithfully but not seeing their harvest during their days in the earth. Some even sacrificed their lives, but they shall now see the fruit of their labors, for it was not in vain. What was sown in tears shall now produce great joy!

Those who sow in tears shall reap in joy. He who continually goes forth weeping, bearing seed for sowing, shall doubtless come again with rejoicing, bringing his sheaves with him (Psalm 126:5-6 NKJV).

Now is the time for every seed to sprout, to grow, and to come to maturity. It is harvest time in the nations. Everywhere My gospel has been preached there shall be a harvest of souls, for it is the season for harvest.

The harvest is plentiful but the laborers are few; therefore, pray for workers to be thrust into the fields that are white with harvest, for I do not want one to be lost. All must be reached.

In this hour there will be a marrying of the evangelists and the disciplers. One will not say to the other, "My mandate is more important and necessary than yours," for there shall be a merging of Mark 16:15 and Matthew 28:19-20 and many ministries will network together for the evangelization and discipleship of nations. Significant and dynamic divine strategies and connections will be granted in this era.

And He said to them, "Go into all the world and preach the gospel to every creature" (Mark 16:15 NKJV).

"Go therefore and make disciples of all the nations, baptizing them in the name of the Father and of the Son and of the Holy Spirit, teaching them to observe all things that I have commanded you; and lo, I am with you always, even to the end of the age." Amen (Matthew 28:19-20 NKJV).

I will raise up new missions organizations that will train evangelists and those who will disciple nations, for there is need of more laborers who are committed and willing to lay down their lives. These laborers will be single-minded and will represent Me in fullness of nature, character, voice, and power. They will carry My authority and represent My interests alone, for they will be My "laid-down lovers."

I am raising up My evangelists and disciplers in every sphere of influence in society. You will find them powerfully impacting government, business and commerce, education, media, arts and entertainment, medical fields, religious and spiritual communities, and families. These ones will not be entangled with the distracting affairs of everyday life but will be focused on Me and their mission to make Me known. They will not present a program, but a Person. They will present *Me* in fullness.

I will also increase My army of intercessors who will pray for My harvest and for My harvesters. They will be tenacious in faith and will grant powerful covering for My laborers. They will give birth to souls, souls, and more souls. Many of My intercessors will find themselves praying for the harvest and for the discipleship of nations with precision and with great burden.

The enemy will attempt to close borders and keep My gospel from reaching the lost, but My people, called by My name, know that I am greater than he that is in the world— they will rise up in faith and I will make a way for them. Nothing will stop My harvest.

Media, Media, Media

I will powerfully use media in this era to proclaim My gospel. Many will be led to Me and discipled through social media and other outlets, for I have set a cloud in mid-heaven that I prevail over and My sickle is in My hand. The eternal gospel will be preached (see Rev. 14:6,14). Do not neglect this distribution funnel—work with deliberation and intentionality while it is yet day; do not delay. More people will be reached with My gospel and discipled through media than other means, for I am blessing this. Prayer meetings, creative presentations of the gospel, training, equipping, mentoring, and pastoring will be hosted on social media. New media and technology platforms will be birthed in this era to host and distribute the proclamation of My gospel in this hour.

Many Will Come to the Lord from False Beliefs

In this era, many Jews, Muslims, Hindus, and those who have served other gods and philosophies will turn to Me. I will also reveal Myself within the Mormon Church and confront, with powerful confirmation, the deception that is holding their people in bondage. Many will lay hold of the truth and be set free. Many will flock to Me.

My Spirit will move upon souls in workplaces, schools, prisons, hospitals, homes, playgrounds, entertainment centers, and marketplaces. Wherever people gather, I will move. It is an era of harvest. *"Put in the sickle, for the harvest is ripe"* (Joel 3:13).

INSIGHTS

The time is now! There is an urgency by the Spirit of Grace to lay the sickle into the ripened harvest fields now and without delay. We must not sleep in the midst of the season of reaping.

> *Do you not say, "There are yet four months, and then comes the harvest"? Behold, I say to you, lift up your eyes and look on the fields, that they are white for harvest* (John 4:35).

> *He who gathers in summer is a son who acts wisely, but he who sleeps in harvest is a son who acts shamefully* (Proverbs 10:5).

Glorious but Treacherous

This hour of great harvest will be glorious, but the opposition and persecution will be exceedingly great in diverse places. In many ways, what the apostles faced in the Book of Acts will look pale in comparison to this hour, but the fruit will be that which has never been seen previously. Not only one nation will be harvested, but there will be great harvests in all nations and amongst every tribe, people group, gender, and age group.

The Laborers

Those who will put their hand to the sickle in this hour will be fully focused and committed to Jesus and His beloved harvest. They will carry His heart, His love, His grace, and His power. They will not be united to the world and its ways but will be completely set apart for the One they serve and for the assignment they have been appointed to by the Spirit. They will not be motivated by a program but by personal passion for the lost. They will be wrapped in favor from on high and will flow in the powerful enabling grace of the Spirit. Every age group will be represented amongst Christ's laborers, and there will be creative ideas for reaching those they carry a burden for.

Message Confirmed

The preaching of the Word will be confirmed by miracles, signs, and wonders (see Mark 16:15-20). The sick will be healed, the demonized will be set free, and the dead will be raised. Many will be visited by face-to-face encounters with Jesus Christ and with angels that He sends to help with the harvest. There will be signs in the heavens and in the earth to confirm the gospel. The power of the Kingdom will be made manifest in this era.

Household Harvest

Many have sown tears in faith-filled intercession for their loved ones, and they will see the reward of their prayers in this era. Entire households will come to know Jesus at the same time, but there will also be great divides and excommunication in families because of family members giving their lives to Jesus. It is an era of extremes.

Discipleship of Nations

The Lord is strategically placing His people in realms of influence in order to disciple nations. There will be an emphasis on reformation in societal spheres, and God will call many of His people like Daniel and Joseph to come alongside of decision makers and influential leaders. They will be influencers of influencers and will see the hand of God move in nations due to their placement.

Thoughts to Ponder

The harvest is plentiful, but the laborers are few. In what areas do you personally and currently see the need for laborers?

Intercession gives birth to the harvest and prepares souls to receive Christ. How can the Body be inspired to engage in prayer for the harvest?

Do you have loved ones who need Christ? Make a list and pray for their salvation.

What area of society (i.e. education, government, business, media, etc.) do you specifically believe needs transformation? Why? Do you feel a specific call to any of these areas?

Do you have a particular nation that God has put on your heart for harvest and discipleship? How can you serve Him in the harvest there?

PRAYER FOR HARVEST

Heavenly Father,

I invite You to increase my love for those who do not yet know You. May Your love-burden become mine. Lead and guide me to be an instrument for carrying Your gospel of the Kingdom to the nations.

In Jesus' name I pray,

Amen.

Chapter
Seventeen

AN ERA OF WARS, RUMORS OF WARS, NATURAL DISASTERS, PLAGUES

For nation will rise against nation, and kingdom against kingdom. And there will be famines, pestilences, and earthquakes in various places.
—MATTHEW 24:7 NKJV

Prophecy

Everything that can be shaken will be shaken, but those who are Mine are of a Kingdom that cannot be shaken. In this era, there will be increased wars, rumors of wars, earthquakes, natural disasters, plagues, and pestilences. Do not fear but pray—draw close to Me. You will find your refuge,

149

peace, strength, health, and provision in Me. For those who know Me there will be no need to fear or to be anxious, for My hand will guide.

When those whom I have created are at peace with Me and are aligned to My ways, there is rest in the land and creation rejoices. But when rebellion toward Me and disobedience to My Word are manifest, there is unrest and turmoil, and creation groans for there is an enemy that takes advantage. He comes to steal, to kill, and to destroy. In the midst of seasons of demonic assault and casualties, *"If My people who are called by My name will humble themselves, and pray and seek My face, and turn from their wicked ways, then I will hear from heaven, and will forgive their sin and heal their land"* (2 Chron. 7:14 NKJV).

In the midst of tensions and shakings, there will be a reset that will take place in the hearts of many. Idols of the heart shall be revealed and they will topple. Many will turn to Me in this hour, for even though the enemy is purposing to destroy lives and destinies of individuals and nations I will work it together for good and there will be a great harvest. He will be defeated, and My great glory will be manifest and spread to the nations.

Fearless warriors will rise up in this era and will go forth as light in the midst of deep and treacherous darkness. They will honor Me and will be willing to lay down their lives for My gospel. Glory shall rise upon them and appear upon them and nations will come to their light and kings to the brightness of their rising (see Isa. 60:1-3).

In the midst of a dark day I will manifest My love, My power, and My provision to all who trust in Me. I will display My goodness for all to see, for I am a righteous God and I am love.

Wickedness is no match for righteousness and deception is no match for truth. Therefore, in the midst of difficult and challenging times, know that I am your hiding place—draw near to Me and turn to Me with all your heart, for I will keep all in perfect peace whose minds are fixed on Me and to those who trust My Word (see Isa. 26:3).

I am a refuge for My people and a strong tower. I will hide My people under the shadow of My wings and will give My angels charge over them. The angel armies of heaven will be released to fight on behalf of truth and righteousness. My people will call, and I will answer. I will be with them in times of trouble and guard them in all their ways, for I am the Lord of Hosts, the Captain of the armies of Heaven.

Do you see people trembling around you? Do you see them gripped with fear? Do not withhold My love and peace from them in their time of distress, but *go* and proclaim the good news of My gospel. I send you forth as My ambassadors of peace, healing, hope, and blessing. You are My benefactors in trying times—you are My heavenly ambassadors. *Go*—for I love them and desire for them to know Me. I long to see them safe in My Kingdom, so *go*. *Go*.

INSIGHTS

Any time that disasters and treacherous circumstances hit the earth, historically we see people coming to the Lord and believers realigning their lives. On September 11, 2001, the Twin Towers in New York were attacked by terrorists and around 3,000 lost their lives and 6,000 were injured in one sweep. Immediately following, the nation was called to prayer and churches were filled to overflowing. Many responded to altar calls for salvation and to receive comfort, healing, and deliverance from fear and loss. Sadly, after a few months when the initial trauma settled, church attendance slowly declined.

The church needs to be "first responders" in times of crisis—ready to meet the needs of the people and especially to preach the good news of the gospel. In difficult times, people's hearts are tender, realizing their dependency on God.

Every generation will face hardships and some generations face more difficulties than others. We know that the enemy comes to steal, kill, and destroy, but Jesus came to give us beautiful and glorious life even in the midst of hardships. It is important to turn to Him and to live for Him, not only in times of attack and severe hardship, but always. The most important posture in life is to live for Jesus—to love Him with all your heart, soul, and strength (see Deut. 6:5). Hardships, although not necessarily authored by God, invite us to live in this posture.

Signs of the End

Although I realize that there are a variety of beliefs, interpretations, and convictions regarding the end of the age, the return of Christ, and the events surrounding us, I believe there are some things to be gleaned by reading the following scriptures as Jesus mentions wars, famines, pestilences, and earthquakes, indicating a warning concerning the times.

The disciples came to Jesus privately, asking, *"What will be the sign of Your coming, and of the end of the age?"* (Matt. 24:3).

Jesus had already come, as He was sitting there speaking with them, so they must have been referring to a subsequent coming. Jesus responded to their question as follows:

> *For nation will rise against nation, and kingdom against kingdom. And there will be famines, pestilences, and earthquakes in various places. All these are the beginning of sorrows.*
>
> *Then they will deliver you up to tribulation and kill you, and you will be hated by all nations for My name's sake. And then many will be offended, will betray one another, and will hate one another. Then many false prophets will rise up and deceive many. And because lawlessness will abound, the love of many will grow cold. But he who endures to the end shall be saved. And this gospel of the kingdom will be preached in all the world as a witness to all the nations, and then the end will come* (Matthew 24:7-14 NKJV).

I encourage you to read the rest of the chapter and the following chapter as there is much to glean from it as Jesus describes the events that mark His return and the end of the age.

The wise response to all that is revealed is simple—we draw close to the Lord and serve Him from a heart of love, devotion, and holy expectation. These signs are a wakeup call for us, not that we should live in fear but in renewed focus and faith. It is like an alarm clock going off in the morning reminding us that it is time to arise. No one wakes up in fear, saying, "Oh no, it's morning!" But we realize it is time to get up and prepare for the day for the new day has begun.

Jesus described some signs (i.e. war, famines, pestilences, earthquakes) that would fore-run the end. Every generation has witnessed signs such as these, and although they might have encountered a time to reset, the "end of the end" has not yet been fulfilled with all the details outlined in various scriptures throughout the New Testament. We do know that His return will come, but we do not know the day and the hour. However, Jesus said that it will come suddenly and yet not without warning.

> *But of that day and hour no one knows, not even the angels of heaven, but My Father only. But as the days of Noah were, so also will the coming of the Son of Man be. For as in the days before the flood, they were eating and drinking, marrying and giving in marriage, until the day that Noah entered the ark, and did not know until the flood came and took them all away, so also will the coming of the Son of Man be* (Matthew 24:36-39 NKJV).

When we hear of wars, rumors of wars, natural disasters, plagues, earthquakes, etc. in this next era, we are to respond with a call to attention and alertness before the Lord, bringing our lives into divine alignment. It is a wakeup call. I am not suggesting that this will necessarily be the "end of the end," but it is a possibility. Are you ready?

This is not intended to be a confrontation of various viewpoints of a believer's eschatology, for I am not in a position to confront, but I have encountered the urgent prompting of the Spirit to not only prophesy the coming of critical events in this next era but also to call us to attention, position, and alignment. Whether there are wars or no wars, our position should be the same. Whether there are earthquakes or no earthquakes, our faith should remain unshakable. Whether there are famines or no famines, Jesus should always be our living bread. Whether there are plagues or no plagues, Jesus should always be our life, our strength—our all.

When we are in Christ, we are blessed, hidden, and protected. He is our present help in time of trouble. When everything else that we leaned on fails us, Jesus keeps and sustains us. He will never leave us or forsake us. Let's always draw near to Him, not out of fear or urgency but because we are fully in love with Him, trusting Him with everything that pertains to us. When we have this blessed assurance, then we are able to confidently go and share His love and salvation with all who do not know Him. A great harvest awaits us in the midst of treacherous times, and a great move of His glory will follow. Let's draw near to Him and delight in His goodness.

Thoughts to Ponder

Do you fear possible disasters, wars, or catastrophic events? If so, in what areas does fear grip you?

How can you eliminate those fears?

Take an inventory of your faith in this hour. Is it strong in the Lord no matter what or does it need strengthening?

Are you confident in God's ability to keep you during crisis? If not, why?

What are some ways you could reach out to others in the midst of crisis?

PRAYER FOR HELP IN TIME OF TROUBLE

Heavenly Father,

You say in Your Word that You are my refuge and strength and a very present help in time of trouble (Ps. 46:1). Fill me with assurance and strength and make me a bold proclaimer of Your love and truth to others in times of crisis. Help me to be Your ambassador of hope to those who suffer. Empower me and mark me as Your servant in dark days that many might be reached for Your glory.

In Jesus' name I pray,

Amen.

Chapter
Eighteen

AN ERA OF MATURING

When I was a child, I used to speak like a child,
think like a child, reason like a child; when I
became a man, I did away with childish things.
—1 CORINTHIANS 13:11

Prophecy

This era calls for commitment, focus, and growth in the lives of My people and My ministers. There is no room for folly and carelessness in this hour, but rather all are invited to cleave to My wisdom and pursue maturity.

From the beginning of creation, I blessed My people with fruitfulness and dominion so that the earth would be stewarded well, but due to the fall, thorns and thistles grew and great labor was required to bring forth fruit from the land. All creation groans and awaits the maturing of My sons and daughters who will free My creation from the curse and influence of sin.

A mighty company of mature believers will be raised up to execute My authority, My will, and My purposes in the earth. Their hearts will be completely Mine and they will not look for favor from man but they will fear Me.

I will raise up My apostles, prophets, evangelists, pastors, and teachers to equip My people for the work of service. They will build up My Body until they attain to the unity of the faith and the knowledge of the Son of God, to a mature man, to the measure of the stature which belongs to the fullness of Christ. As a result, My people will no longer be children, tossed here and there by waves and carried about by every wind of doctrine, by the trickery of men, by craftiness in deceitful scheming; but speaking the truth in love, they will grow up in all aspects into Him who is the head, even Christ, from whom the whole body, being fitted and held together by what every joint supplies, according to the proper working of each individual part, which causes the growth of the body for the building up of itself in love (see Eph. 4:12-16).

My mature ones will be motivated by love and will move forward in obedience to Me, and they will be fearless. They will know when to speak and when not to speak. They will know when to act and when not to act. They will walk in step with Me and will fulfill My purposes.

Through many trials and testings, I have perfected them. They have submitted to the fire of My purging and refinement, and they have kept the faith. Many in this hour will rise out of a place of obscurity and come into visibility. Many who have been silent will now speak, and many who have not moved will now create movement.

This is an era for maturing. It is an era for putting away childish things. It is an era when all must make careful decisions and choices. I am calling for the maturity of My Body into the full measure of My stature.

INSIGHTS

I love Romans 8:19-23 in Dr. Brian Simmons' *The Passion Translation*. This portion highlights the identity and mandate of the "mature children of God."

The entire universe is standing on tiptoe, yearning to see the unveiling of God's glorious sons and daughters! For against its will the universe itself has had to endure the empty futility resulting from the consequences of human sin. But now, with eager expectation, all creation longs for freedom from its slavery to decay and to experience with us the wonderful freedom coming to God's children. To this day we are aware of the universal agony and groaning of creation, as if it were in the contractions of labor for childbirth. And it's not just creation. We who have already experienced the firstfruits of the Spirit also inwardly groan as we passionately long to experience our full status as God's sons and daughters— including our physical bodies being transformed.

In the natural lives of human beings, we can observe five stages of development.

Infancy

As an infant, you are completely dependent on your parents or caregivers for food, bathing, management of elimination of waste, and nurture. You drink milk and are not ready for solid foods. You do not communicate well yet, but you can cry when you are hungry or need changing or have pain and you can coo and smile in response to loving communication.

Toddler

As a toddler, you have learned to feed yourself, drink from your cup, walk, and you have begun speaking words using a simple and limited vocabulary. Although you are learning these limited life skills, you continue to be dependent on parents or caregivers and are not held responsible for tasks such as household chores.

Tender-Aged

From age four to thirteen, your body frame is growing, your features are becoming more pronounced, and your personality is forming. You are growing in communication and social skills and you are learning to live as part of a family, able to take responsibly for assigned tasks. You are growing in your ability to exercise logic and wisdom. You are engaged in academic growth and accelerated life skills.

Teen

In this phase you have entered puberty. Your body matures in many ways and you now have the ability to procreate. Although you lack experience in life, you are now making more important choices and are able to begin taking on adult responsibilities and learning life lessons from these experiences. You look to parents for guidance and in most cases continue to be under their legal authority.

Adult

You are now fully matured physically and legally and are morally responsible for your actions.

In our spiritual growth there are five stages of development also.

In the New Testament, there are five different Greek words that are used to describe stages of development in the Christian life. They are *Nepios, Paidion, Teknon, Huios*, and *Teleios*. Our goal is to grow into maturity in Christ as a mature son/daughter of God.

Nepios

In *Strong's Concordance*, the word *nepios* refers to an infant, a little child, a minor, not of age (#G3516). Nepios is metaphorically used for childish, untaught, unskilled, or immature.

A "Nepios Christian" could be described as being born again of the Spirit but like an infant in the faith. They might still be in bondage under the elements of the world (see Gal. 4:1-3), led by carnal desires and passions (see 1 Cor. 3:1-4), and are not yet mature or skilled in the understanding and application of the Word. They need the pure milk of the Word in order to grow (see 1 Pet. 2:2; Heb. 5:4-5).

Paidion

In *Strong's Concordance*, the word *paidion* refers to a young child— a young child of tender age, younger than twelve—for boys, prior to their bar-mitzvah (#G3813).

A "Paidion Christian" is learning to have meaningful relationship with their heavenly Father and learning to submit to His will and discipline. They will find a battle between flesh and spirit as they are in a great stage of formation and development. One of the precious characteristics of a "Paidion" is their innocent, childlike humility, dependency, and faith that Jesus described in Matthew 18:1-4.

Teknon

In *Strong's Concordance*, the word *teknon* gives the understanding of a disciple or a child of their teachers who instruct and nourish the minds of their pupils and form their character (#G5043). In comparison to a natural stage of life in western culture, the Teknon would be a teenager who is able to understand what life offers and enter into preparation and equipping.

A "Teknon Christian" has grown in understanding and skill, but is not fully matured in character or the implementation of wisdom.

Huios

In *Strong's Concordance*, the word *huios* means "those who revere God as their father, pious worshipers of God, those who in character and life resemble God, those who are governed by the Spirit of God, repose the same calm and joyful trust in God which children do their parents" (#G5207).

A "Huios Christian" has reached maturity in Christ and reflects the character and nature of Jesus Christ. They are obedient to the Father's will, promptings, and actions and they are led by the Spirit as Christ was. They resist the flesh as we find in Romans 8:12-14:

> *So then, brethren, we are under obligation, not to the flesh,*
> *to live according to the flesh—for if you are living according*

to the flesh, you must die; but if by the Spirit you are putting to death the deeds of the body, you will live. For all who are being led by the Spirit of God, these are sons [huios] of God.

They manifest the fruit of the Spirit as found in Galatians 5:22-25:

But the fruit of the Spirit is love, joy, peace, patience, kindness, goodness, faithfulness, gentleness, self-control; against such things there is no law. Now those who belong to Christ Jesus have crucified the flesh with its passions and desires. If we live by the Spirit, let us also walk by the Spirit.

In addition, the "Huios Christian" will use their God-given gifts, abilities, and maturity for the purpose of helping all believers also achieve maturity and to live as holy, mature sons and daughters of God (see Eph. 4:7-24).

The *huios* stage of development is when true Kingdom leaders arise, as mature men and women of God. They are mature, knowing the difference between good and evil; they have discernment and are experienced and developed in their gifts and callings, bringing unity to the Body of Christ. They live holy lives beyond reproach on a consistent basis. Love is their motive for all they do, and although they embrace the gifts of the Holy Spirit, they have made love their greatest aim (see 1 Cor. 14:1). They are known for their love, excellence of character, unwavering faith, and pure commitment to God and His Word.

Many "Huios Christians" will arise and be made manifest in this era.

Teleios

In *Strong's Concordance*, the word *teleios* means:

1. brought to its end, finished

2. wanting nothing necessary to completeness

3. perfect

4. that which is perfect

5. consummate human integrity and virtue

6. of men

7. full grown, adult, of full age, mature (#G5046)

The "Teleios Christian" looks exactly like Jesus and has perfectly transformed and matured into His likeness. As we yield to the Spirit of God, this glorious work of unveiling takes place. We grow through His Spirit of grace, truth, and glory from Nepios, to Paidion, to Teknon, to Huios, and to Teleios.

> So then, my beloved, just as you have always obeyed, not as in my presence only, but now much more in my absence, work out your salvation with fear and trembling; for it is God who is at work in you, both to will and to work for His good pleasure (Philippians 2:12-13).

Let us yield afresh to the Spirit who is bringing us into completion, and may the mature children of God truly arise.

> But we all, with unveiled face, beholding as in a mirror the glory of the Lord, are being transformed into the same image from glory to glory, just as from the Lord, the Spirit (2 Corinthians 3:18).

Thoughts to Ponder

Do you believe there is a need for the Body of Christ to mature in this era? Why?

Imagine the Body of Christ in full maturity. Describe what that would look like if it were to be manifest in this era.

What areas of immaturity have you seen in the Body of Christ in general?

What stage of development in the spirit do you see yourself at this time?

What is the Spirit speaking to you about your personal growth and maturity?

PRAYER FOR MATURITY

Heavenly Father,

I want to mature so I can be just like Jesus and manifest His glorious nature, authority, and power. Have Your way in me and transform me by Your Spirit from glory to glory.

In Jesus' name I pray,

Amen.

Chapter
Nineteen

AN ERA OF INCREASED DIVINE ENCOUNTERS AND ANGELIC VISITATION

I was in the Spirit on the Lord's day, and I heard behind me a loud voice like the sound of a trumpet. ...Then I turned to see the voice that was speaking with me. And having turned I saw.
—REVELATION 1:10,12

Prophecy

In this era there will be an increase of divine encounters and angelic visitations. Spiritual sensitivity will increase in My people to the reality of the invisible realm of My Kingdom and spiritual conversations and testimonies will be more acceptable in camps where they were once rejected. The spiritual senses of My people will open up and many will see open visions and hear audible sounds. New levels of authentic God-encounters will be experienced in this era.

I am releasing My angel armies in this era to wage war against the devil's attacks and deceptions, and I will give My angels charge concerning you, to guard you in all your ways (see Ps. 91:11). My angelic host will protect you, direct you, and communicate My messages to you for they are *"all ministering spirits, sent out to render service for the sake of those who will inherit salvation"* (Heb. 1:14).

This era will host strategic spiritual visitations and encounters, for I will deliver messages of divine knowledge, wisdom, and understanding that will grant insights not yet understood by man. Divine intelligence will be granted through visitation. Even as I met with Abraham, Moses, Daniel, Elijah, Mary, John, and others in order to reveal My divine will and purpose, I will grant many such strategic encounters in this era with those whom I have set apart for special assignments.

It is important in this season to seek the things above where I am seated, setting your minds on things above rather than on the things of the earth. For you are seated with Me in heavenly places and your life is hidden in Me.

Children

Many children in the younger generation will have encounters in My presence and will see into the realm of the spirit. They will be visited by angels. When they share their encounters, it is important to believe them, for they will share from their heart. Encourage children to grow in My realms of the supernatural. They will possess understanding beyond their years, for it will come from Me.

The Arts

In this era, I will release heavenly art, music, and performing arts expressions. Numbers will testify of learning their skills in My presence and in the heavenly dimensions of My Kingdom. Without natural education, they will far surpass in skill those who have been trained in their skill through natural instruction and practice. Much of the art in this era will depict that which is seen in the spirit and will be marked in history. Prophetic art, dance, and music will increase.

Photography

I will cause many to capture supernatural appearances through photography and videography in this era. The distribution of these images will be for signs and wonders in the earth and will cause many to look to Me, but there will also be counterfeits who will arise.

Counterfeits

These counterfeits will look for attention and fame. Beware of them, for they will attempt to deceive many in order to gain a following, and their hidden motive is for financial gain and advantage.

This era is a supernatural era. As you experience an increase of divine, supernatural, and angelic encounters, the enemy will raise up his counterfeit forces and signs and wonders. Do not be deceived by him. True encounters will exalt Me and not man.

Look to Me and look for Me.

INSIGHTS

Authentic Christ-centered spiritual encounters are life-giving and usually very significant, even historically significant. I love meditating on the biblical examples of supernatural encounters such as Moses meeting I AM at the burning bush; Elijah being fed by an angel; Daniel being visited by the angel Gabriel; Ezekiel beholding the Man of Fire; Peter, James and John beholding Jesus, Moses, and Elijah on the Mount of Transfiguration; Jesus appearing to the disciples in a room without entering through the door; and many others.

Supernatural encounters are common in the scriptures and have become more common in the last three decades. It wasn't long ago, however, when the majority in the Body of Christ were not open to the reality of supernatural revelation and encounters being experienced today in the lives of believers. After Jesus left the earth, we were given His Holy Spirit to lead and guide us into all truth and to disclose to us what is ours in Jesus (see John 16:13-15). The Holy Spirit will never lead us astray or introduce us to anything false. We need to trust Him to lead us into valid, God-given revelation and encounters.

Let's examine what the apostle Paul penned to the church at Corinth when he was encouraging them to trust spiritual revelation and encounter that was born and led of the Spirit.

Now we have received, not the spirit of the world, but the Spirit who is from God, so that we may know the things freely given to us by God, which things we also speak, not in words taught by human wisdom, but in those taught by the Spirit, combining spiritual thoughts with spiritual words.

But a natural man does not accept the things of the Spirit of God, for they are foolishness to him; and he cannot under-stand them, because they are spiritually appraised. But he who is spiritual appraises all things (1 Corinthians 2:12-15).

In this era, there will be an escalation of focus on the supernatural and an increase of actual supernatural visitations and angelic encounters. It is important to examine the scriptures and invite the Holy Spirit to give fresh revelation and insight concerning this subject. It is time for the church to mature in our understanding of these things, or we could be in danger of becoming the same as any other benevolent organization or religion.

Many secular organizations do good and value integrity, care for others, and show compassion even as the church does. Most religions also carry similar values. What makes Christianity different is that we believe God is all powerful and that His people are empowered by Him to do the works that Jesus did in the earth and even greater works (see John 14:12). If we eliminate the power of God and spiritual encounter, we are no different.

Jesus lived, He died, and He was resurrected from the dead. His disciples and others saw Him following His resurrection. He birthed our new covenant in power and not in philosophy or empty words. When He was about to ascend, He said to His disciples:

But you will receive power when the Holy Spirit has come upon you; and you shall be My witnesses both in Jerusalem, and in all Judea and Samaria, and even to the remotest part of the earth (Acts 1:8).

We are actually warned by Paul concerning lack of power in his letter to Timothy when he spoke of the last days:

*But realize this, that in the last days difficult times will come. For men will be lovers of self, lovers of money, boastful, arrogant, revilers, disobedient to parents, ungrateful, unholy, unloving, irreconcilable, malicious gossips, without self-control, brutal, haters of good, treacherous, reckless, conceited, lovers of pleasure rather than lovers of God, **holding to a form of godliness, although they have denied its power; avoid such men as these** (2 Timothy 3:1-5).*

We are actually instructed in the scriptures to avoid those who deny the power and only hold to a form of godliness. Supernatural power and encounters define the church and yet so many deny them. Jesus Himself said that signs *will* follow those who believe (see Mark 16:17). If we believe, we can expect the supernatural!

God wants you to experience Him and His Kingdom. Get positioned for a great era of accelerated supernatural encounters and angelic visitation.

Thoughts to Ponder

God wants you to encounter His supernatural power and Kingdom. Do you believe this?

Do you have any fears regarding the supernatural? If so, describe.

Do you have favorite stories in the Bible that display supernatural visitation and encounter? Describe.

Have you ever sensed the presence of or seen an angel sent by God? Describe.

Make a wish list of divine encounters you would like to receive.

PRAYER FOR DIVINE ENCOUNTERS AND ANGELIC VISITATIONS

Heavenly Father,

Stir hunger in me for You and for supernatural encounters in Your Kingdom. I long to embrace all that You desire to give me. I open my heart to receive from You alone. Increase my spiritual sensitivity and receptivity to Your Holy Spirit in this hour.

In Jesus' name I pray,

Amen.

Chapter
Twenty

AN ERA OF BOUNTIFUL, SUPERNATURAL PROVISION

Your kingdom come. Your will be done, on earth as it is in heaven. Give us this day our daily bread.
—MATTHEW 6:10-11

Prophecy

Know that I am a God of abundant provision and I delight to bless My children. In no way will I leave My children without provision or support when they trust in Me alone to supply all their needs.

In this coming era, I will empower those whose hearts are completely Mine to enjoy great abundance, for I am El Shaddai, the God of more than enough, and I will reveal

Myself as El Shaddai in this era to My people. I have granted My people the power to make wealth, but there is a warning that must be heeded, for the love of money and material things is crouching at the door of men's hearts and its desire is to have them. The love of money is the root of many forms of evil and must be avoided. Money has become an idol to many, but:

> "Once more (it is a little while) I will shake heaven and earth, the sea and dry land; and I will shake all nations, and they shall come to the Desire of All Nations, and I will fill this temple with glory," says the Lord of hosts. "The silver is Mine, and the gold is Mine," says the Lord of hosts. "The glory of this latter temple shall be greater than the former," says the Lord of hosts. "And in this place I will give peace," says the Lord of hosts" (Haggai 2:6-9 NKJV).

My glory, My wealth will be made manifest in the lives of My people in this era as they look to Me. The latter wealth of My house shall be greater than the former, but I will shake everything that can be shaken so that what cannot be shaken will remain. All that is in Me and of Me will remain.

When you see economies shake, do not fear, but look to Me. Follow Me one day at a time and watch what I will do for you. Do not be anxious as to what you shall eat, or what you shall wear, or where you should live, for I do not want you to fear but to trust Me as I have great provision awaiting you.

Do not be moved either when economies recover and flourish, for they shall rise and fall, but My provision will be steadfast, for My economy is always stable. I am the stability of your times. Do not look to the world or its systems to provide for you, for I am your Provider and even though I will command the world to bless you, always remember that you are not of the world.

I am the God who caused bread to fall from heaven to feed My people in the wilderness. I caused water to flow out of a rock and My peopled lacked for nothing year after year, for I provided well for them. Even though I daily revealed My abundance, they failed to acknowledge My goodness and started to long for Egypt again with its leeks and garlic even though I had separated them unto Myself and delivered them from the power of the very system that oppressed them. They were My covenant people, but they forgot who they were and they failed to gaze upon Me and acknowledge My goodness. Beware lest you fall into the same ensnarement of the enemy's deception. I will always provide, and I am always good.

You will see My supernatural intervention bring blessing to you as you wait upon Me, for you belong to My Kingdom and My Kingdom is not of this world. You are in the world but you are not of it—you belong to Me. Remember this.

Your provisional well-being is not for only a moment but for all your days, so do not fear but stir expectation and dream big with Me, for you will see My promises unfold and manifest in your life. I will do exceedingly abundantly above all you can ask or think according to the power that works within you (see Eph. 3:20). Your key is to believe in Me and to believe in My promises, for I will not and cannot fail. It is only when you turn your attention away from Me and when you fail to align with My teachings concerning My Kingdom's economy that you will fall short. I have made it easy for all to prosper, but true prosperity flows from your alignment to Me and My ways and true prosperity is greater than material possessions.

> Therefore I say to you, do not worry about your life, what you will eat or what you will drink; nor about your body, what you will put on. Is not life more than food and the body more than clothing? ...For after all these things the Gentiles seek. For your heavenly Father knows that you need all these things. But seek first the kingdom of God and His righteousness, and all these things shall be added to you. Therefore do not worry about tomorrow, for tomorrow will worry about its own things (Matthew 6:25,32-34 NKJV).

I promise to supply all your need according to My riches in glory (see Phil. 4:19). Rejoice, rise up in faith and expectation, for your days are numbered with My goodness. Faith is My Kingdom's currency. In this era, you will grow in faith and secure My promises.

INSIGHTS

Most individuals, whether Christians or non-Christians, are consumed with a focus on material possessions and financial well-being. Without realizing it, more attention is often given to these issues than our devotion to the Lord. In order to enjoy divine glory and the provision within it, there needs to be divine alignment and order. In this new era, the Lord is going to help His people align. You are going to your next level of experiencing God's abundance so you definitely want to be positioned for the best years of your life. The following are some areas of consideration.

Reset Our Focus on Jesus Himself

When we find ourselves distracted with longings or anxiety concerning provision or earthly possessions, it is an indication that we have lost our focus on the most important foundation in life—*Jesus Himself.* This does not mean thinking about Him for a flashing moment here and there throughout our day, but actually connecting with Him and living in union with Him. He is not a mere influence or power, He is a person. He is Emanuel—"God With Us." And He is waiting and longing to have a deep and meaningful relationship with us. When we have Jesus, we have everything, because "Jesus + Nothing = Everything We Need." It is so easy to lose focus, so let's consciously choose to refocus when we find ourselves distracted.

When you find yourself struggling with apprehension concerning your needs, it is a sign that you have shifted your focus from Jesus onto provisional issues. When you turn your attention back to Jesus as your Provider and Lover of your soul, you will find peace, and that is the place where God's hand can move.

Jesus addressed His disciples regarding the issues of fear and anxiety. Look at how He taught them to shift their focus.

> *For this reason I say to you, **do not be worried about your** *
> ***life**, as to what you will eat or what you will drink; nor for *
> *your body, as to what you will put on. Is not life more than *
> *food, and the body more than clothing? Look at the birds of *

the air, that they do not sow, nor reap nor gather into barns, and yet your heavenly Father feeds them. Are you not worth much more than they? **And who of you by being worried can add a single hour to his life?** *And why are you worried about clothing? Observe how the lilies of the field grow; they do not toil nor do they spin, yet I say to you that not even Solomon in all his glory clothed himself like one of these. But if God so clothes the grass of the field, which is alive today and tomorrow is thrown into the furnace, will He not much more clothe you? You of little faith!* **Do not worry then, saying, "What will we eat?" or "What will we drink?" or "What will we wear for clothing?"** *For the Gentiles eagerly seek all these things;* **for your heavenly Father knows that you need all these things. But seek first His kingdom and His righteousness, and all these things will be added to you.** *So do not worry about tomorrow; for tomorrow will care for itself. Each day has enough trouble of its own* (Matthew 6:25-34).

Contentment

We live in a society that is very entitled, and the world's marketing and promotion industries are always suggesting that we do not possess what we need or desire, and then they often pressure us to believe we can't live well without what they are offering. Most of today's marketers are trained to intentionally stir discontentment in their targets to show them how much they absolutely need what they don't have.

We are always being pushed to go for the "more." While there is nothing wrong with having dreams, goals, and desires, we must be careful not to be driven to fulfill the flesh through dissatisfaction. Let's look at what Paul shared with Timothy.

> *Now godliness with contentment is great gain. For we brought nothing into this world, and it is certain we can carry nothing out. And having food and clothing, with these we shall be content. But those who desire to be rich fall into temptation and a snare, and into many foolish and harmful lusts which drown men in destruction and perdition. For the love of money is a root of all kinds of evil, for which some have strayed from the faith in their greediness, and pierced themselves through with many sorrows* (1 Timothy 6:6-10 NKJV).

During a time when my husband and I were learning to live by faith with no visible means of financial support, we went through very challenging times when our faith was stretched daily. One day, I went to the fridge to get milk for my children's cereal and there was not a drop to be found. I might have woken up on the wrong side of the bed, but I remember murmuring, grumbling, and complaining before God for the lack we were living in. After I had ranted for a while, He spoke to me clearly about being thankful for what He had given us. I realized in that moment that I indeed had so much to be grateful for. After all, the boys had cereal, just no milk, and even though I did not have a dime to go out and buy milk, I knew that we were blessed to have so many things. I went to the sink and turned on the water taps, thanking God for the available water we had. I thanked Him for the home we lived in and that we had lights and heat and even a phone. I opened the cupboards and thanked Him for the few cans of food on the shelf and for the plates we had to eat food from when we had it. After about twenty minutes of praising and thanking Him for all His blessings, a deep and rich contentment filled my heart. It was so peaceful and beautiful. I was satisfied and blessed. While I was enjoying that settled feeling, my doorbell rang. When I opened the door, a woman was standing there whom I did not know very well and in her arms was a gallon of fresh farm milk. She said, "I was just at the farm buying my milk and I felt the Lord prompt me to buy you a gallon. Can you use it?"

I was so richly blessed, not just because of the wonderful provision of the milk, but because I realized that contentment truly brings great gain. It not only fills you with supernatural peace, but it opens the way for the hand of God to intervene on your behalf.

Contentment with thanksgiving is an antidote for the ungodly entitlement we see operating in the world today.

Sowing and Reaping

If you are going to be positioned for Kingdom abundance, then we are to first align with Kingdom economy. God so beautifully reveals the principles in His Word for us.

What we sow, we reap. God gave mankind a perpetual covenant through Noah that is found in Genesis 8:22. He promised that as long as the earth remains there will be a time to sow and a time to reap. There will always be a corresponding harvest that follows a period of sowing. We should always be sowing into the next season and never withholding "seed."

Our first and primary sowing is unto God Himself. We honor Him with the tithe (ten percent) of our income. That is the most precious seed of all. It represents our worship, devotion, and honor and the promises that accompany it are massive.

> *"Bring all the tithes into the storehouse, that there may be food in My house, and try Me now in this," says the Lord of hosts, "if I will not open for you the windows of heaven and pour out for you such blessing that there will not be room enough to receive it. And I will rebuke the devourer for your sakes, so that he will not destroy the fruit of your ground, nor shall the vine fail to bear fruit for you in the field," says the Lord of hosts; "and all nations will call you blessed, for you will be a delightful land," says the Lord of hosts* (Malachi 3:10-12 NKJV).

Other sowing opportunities can include your giving to the poor, to special projects and needs, and even sowing into future desires. We know one thing for certain—what we sow, we reap, and we will always reap more than we sow. This is not just for provisional realms but in every realm of life. Look at the powerful insights and promises Paul shares with us in regard to sowing.

> *But this I say: He who sows sparingly will also reap sparingly, and he who sows bountifully will also reap bountifully. So let each one give as he purposes in his heart, not grudgingly or of necessity; for God loves a cheerful giver. And God is able to make all grace abound toward you, that you, always having all sufficiency in all things, may have an abundance for every good work. As it is written:*
>
> *"He has dispersed abroad, He has given to the poor; His righteousness endures forever."*

Now may He who supplies seed to the sower, and bread for food, supply and multiply the seed you have sown and increase the fruits of your righteousness, while you are enriched in everything for all liberality, which causes thanksgiving through us to God. For the administration of this service not only supplies the needs of the saints, but also is abounding through many thanksgivings to God (2 Corinthians 9:6-12 NKJV).

Let's get positioned for an era of great abundance.

Thoughts to Ponder

Jesus gives life in abundance. What areas of life do you believe this abundance refers to?

Do you have any fears regarding provision for the coming days? Describe.

Are these fears based on lies about the nature of God? If so, identify the lies and cast them down, replacing them with truth.

Dream big with God and ponder what your abundant life will look like in this next era. Journal your thoughts and expectations.

Pray about sowing intentionally and consistently into your future. What action would you like to take?

PRAYER FOR ABUNDANT PROVISION

Heavenly Father,

You are so very good and have promised me abundant life. Help me to always remember Jesus and His faithfulness when I am tempted to worry or to be anxious about provision. Help me to turn to Him with all my heart and fill me with an increased measure of faith and conviction regarding Your abundant provision.

In Jesus' name I pray,

Amen.

About
Patricia King

Patricia King is a respected apostolic minister of the gospel, successful business owner, and an inventive entrepreneur. She is an accomplished itinerant speaker, author, television host, media producer, and ministry network overseer who has given her life fully to Jesus Christ and to His Kingdom's advancement in the earth. She is the founder of Patricia King Ministries and co-founder of XPmedia.com.